Coringa Drive

BONNIE CORDOVA

D1739145

.

For Hannah and Rosie

CONTENTS

PROLOGUE

I grew up on Coringa Drive, and the name sounded chewy, yet bouncy with a robust finish. It occurred to me when I was about halfway through writing this book that it might make me look more literary if I actually knew what Coringa meant.

After procrastinating for a month I pushed up my sleeves, closed Facebook, and Googled "Coringa."

The first thing that popped up on my screen were images of the Joker from the Batman comics. It turned out that "Coringa" in Portuguese literally means "joker."

I thought, "Okay, this can represent my brother Bob, when he was supposed to babysit, or an image from the

McCarthy era representing the blacklist." I thought of these things but they didn't gel. What I had to realize was that the Coringa is me with a knack for finding humor in pain.

The next link I found belonged to the Coringa-Herald Nature Reserve, located in the Coral Sea Islands Territory off the coast of Australia. The islands were lovely, but I decided to continue my search. Finally, I discovered that Wikipedia had the most compelling entry on "Coringa":

"**Coringa** is a tiny village off the East Godavari district, in Andhra Pradesh, India. In 1789, a cyclone hit, causing a strong storm surge which killed 20,000. On November 16, 1839 another disastrous cyclone struck east India with terrible winds and another giant storm surge. Once again, Coringa was destroyed."

I had two divorces, from Tim and from Anthony, but how pretentious is that to compare divorce to storm surges that killed thousands of people? When I was in the middle of them I would have argued my case, but now I see it differently. Maybe it was a psychic, emotional storm surge that wiped me out twice, but that's not what this memoir is about. This memoir is about random pieces from my life. I just caught them. They didn't surge at me—they leapt at me.

Coringa Drive is divided into four sections. The first is "Arkin," the name I inherited from my father, my maiden name. The second is "Robertson," my new last name when I married Tim. I loved that name. I got to stop being ethnic for a while; that is, until a friend of Tim's father, a Baptist minister, tried to convert me. I also got to stop being part of my family. There are many famous people in my family, and I became a free agent. I traveled incognito. You can go anywhere with the name "Robertson".

"Castelluccio" was my third name when I married Anthony and became Italian. I spent a lot of time spelling that one, but loved the sound of it, and didn't want to give it up when I married Amado. Amado felt that it wouldn't be appropriate to keep, so I decided to adopt my fourth, and hopefully last, name: "Cordova." I'm Mexican now.

I didn't know how it would feel to have this, my fourth name, but I came to realize that no matter what last name I use, it's the same me, whatever that is: the same center, the same feelings. I'm still Jewish, I still have the same family. I'm older now than when I was with the other names. I'm less hormone-driven, less emotional.

I can do "Cordova."

*References

Murali, D. (2005). "This storm is like a lasting match." The Hindu Business Line. Retrieved 6 June 2010.

Reid, William (1849). *The progress of the development of the law of storms....* J. Weale. p. 105.

Balfour, Edward (1885). *The cyclopaedia of India and of eastern and southern Asia.* **2**. B. Quaritch. p. 125.

Chambers, William (1851). *Chambers's Papers for the people.* p. 15.

ARKIN

Once I wanted to be a poet

Once I wanted to be a poet,
To be fairly well known
In certain circles,

Thin, of course,
Small spaces being my food.

I'd be poignant and quirky.
An original
(like other poets).

I'd have no need for makeup.
People would see my beauty
In the way I brought them the agony
Of leaves,
And the unbearable perfection
Of noon.

1 MY HOME TOWN

Highland Park didn't seem like it was in the middle of a city. There were fields and hills and trees. I didn't wear shoes from June to September. I was black from being in the sun all the time. I didn't know any other color to be. I had bathing suit lines until January or later. We didn't know about sunscreen, and we climbed over the hill to Yosemite Pool every day in the summer. We used to take turns breathing in the smog and chlorine, cough, and then laugh.

My mother put my older brother, Bob, in charge. In the pool he would try to drown me. He would pull me around by my feet, and I'd dogpaddle with my hands, but sometimes I couldn't keep my head up because he was pulling me too fast. He was very playful about it, but I would get a lot of chlorine up my nose, and swallow it. I felt that the drowning was real. Sometimes having my brother in charge felt like a near-death experience.

It was cold in the dressing room, and it echoed. There were puddles on the floor from wet suits. Later, I had dreams about having a baby there . . . it would just fall out. The floors were concrete and everything smelled like chlorine. We had to take a shower before we went in the pool. The water was cold, no matter how hot the day was. Sometimes we got money for ice cream for afterwards, when the pool closed. Once I didn't have any money and I remember sticking my hand all the way up inside the ice cream vending machine and pulling out an ice cream. We were very hungry, and it was a long hike home. It was my introduction to crime.

I went to nursery school at Yosemite Park. The teacher was Ms. Whittaker. She had black hair that was braided and wrapped in a circle on top of her head. One day my mother and I showed up early and I saw her brushing out her hair. It was breathtakingly long and shiny. Then she braided it and wrapped it around her head. I never knew how she had been able to make that circle up there. It was amazing. It was like watching someone shape-shifting. She transformed from something wild and beautiful into Just My Teacher, something functional and utilitarian.

The girl who painted next to me made a cool picture on her easel. The body was just a large "A". I thought that was a great idea. So I tried to imitate it but nobody seemed very impressed. I made Play-Doh nests and eggs, just how my mother taught me. First I rolled out the mud-green Play-Doh with my hands until it looked like a snake, then I coiled it into a nest; then I made little eggs with the remaining pieces, and put them in the nest that smelled like my hands and the room. Play-Doh smell, tempera paints, and finger-painting . . . paint mixed with starch and smeared on shiny paper. It was heaven.

"We need to share." That's what Ms. Whittaker always said to us, and it was fine, until one day when I wheeled the tricycle to the top of a hill. I liked to ride it down, fast, with my feet off the pedals. That was my introduction to "extreme sports." On this particular day a boy named Matthew tried to take the tricycle away from me. "We need to share," said Mrs. Whittaker when she came running up the hill to see what the disturbance was about. "You got to take the tricycle up the hill so Matthew gets to take it down!" I wish I'd had a lawyer with me at times like that. I couldn't defend myself. I was mute with disbelief. And I've had my share of tricycle moments and gone limp in the face of injustice.

Sometimes we went to the wading pool on Figueroa. That seemed exotic. Foreign territory. The pool was shallow and the water was warm. I liked to pee in it. I liked to pee pretty much everywhere: in my bed, in my pants, in sleeping bags. Carolyn La Grasta was my peeing buddy. When I went home with her after school I'd borrow a pair of her heavy cotton underwear, and when she came to my house she'd borrow mine. They were always stained and slightly gray.

Eric Partlow wet the bed, too. He actually had rubber sheets on his bed, which I thought was smart. We got to sleep on his brother Gene's bed because it was a double bed. Gene was a saint. He was always nice to me, even though he was my brother's friend. Once, though, they made Eric and me kiss on the lips. We thought it was stupid, but we did it for the attention.

Eric had a planetarium that you could project on the ceiling. I remember lying there late at night in the dark room while he identified the constellations for me with a magical light pointer. He always used to be able to make me laugh. That served him well when we competed at games like tetherball. He would engage me, then when I started laughing he'd come in for the kill.

The Partlows had a dog that was half-collie, half-German shepherd, named Pogo. Once when I was walking across the hill to their house, Pogo knocked me down and tried to have sex with me. I was scared; I couldn't get up until a neighbor came running and pulled him off.

We had community fireworks for the Fourth of July. Oxy (Occidental College) had bonfires every year, and we'd run around the field and catch the ashes. On other Fourth of Julys, we'd sit up on top of Kite Hill and watch the fireworks over Eagle Rock High School.

Flat Top was the Partlows' hill. It was by their house. Ours was Kite Hill. Noni lived down the hill past the chicken coop that became a rabbit hutch, then a pigeon coop. Our property was bordered by eucalyptus trees. When you walked on the acorns (we knew they weren't actually acorns, but that's what we called them) they smelled wonderful. Like home. They were not fun to walk on within bare feet, though. Past the trees was a hill, then a vacant lot, then Noni's house. Noni's house was normal. It had sidewalks, and traditional furniture. When you walked into our house you entered my father's studio, decorated with a secondhand couch and a bombing chart from WWII for a coffee table. Noni had a clean, powder-blue bedroom with a canopy bed and a fuzzy white rug. I wanted a room like that. Mine had brown asphalt tile on the floor, and a brown pegboard partition separating me and my brother, Bob. There was a hand-me-down blue-gray desk, and it was always messy. I had paper doll pageants all over the floor, and I didn't want to put them away, because they were in the middle of something, and I didn't want them to forget where they were.

Mrs. Jones lived to the right. She was a Holy Roller, my mother said. She threw her garbage out the window and brought flowers one day to give to my grandparents, to convert them to Christianity. She had long, gray hair and rolled it up into a bun. When I saw it down I thought of a Halloween witch, but she didn't have the face of a Halloween witch. Her face was normal.

Mrs. Fisher lived on the other side of my grandparents. She had been an exotic dancer. She didn't have any kids. She had a pink satin love seat that was loved by my dog Blinker. We didn't know why Blinker was getting so fat, until we found out that Mrs. Fisher and four other neighbors were feeding her.

I remember my dad rescuing Mrs. Fisher, twice. Once there was a garter snake in her pigeon coop. At least somebody said it was a garter snake. My dad went running up the hill with a shovel to kill it because it was eating the pigeons, and I followed him up to watch, which was a mistake. I saw what looked like feathers and guts all over the coop, but I didn't watch him kill the snake. Another time my dad went running up the hill to Mrs. Fisher's house to rescue her because she got her hair caught in the ringer of the washing machine.

Davey Gonzalez lived on the other side of Mrs. Fisher, right next to the Oxy ball field, and Mrs. Rigney lived behind my parents' bedroom. She kept a room full of birds, and had one bedroom for summer, and one for winter. She had steps going down to Range View. That's how I went to school.

We had a cesspool. It would back up and stink terribly. It happened during my birthday party once. My dad really got his nasty face when he'd have to go down there with a shovel. That was one good thing about being a girl. I never had to help him with that. At least ours didn't back up into the bathtub, like the Partlows' did. They had a different kind of cesspool, but it was one other thing that created a bond between us, besides the fact that they were Communists too, and they all played the guitar, and they had a kid for each of my brothers, and one for me, so we could trade and it would be fair. I'd go to their house; Gene would go to mine, and vice versa.

The Wecklers lived on a hill between our house and the Partlows, but when the blacklist came, Joe Weckler killed himself. Robbie, another friend, couldn't play with me anymore because we were Communists. Some other kids at school stopped coming over too, but I didn't know if it was just because they didn't like me. Eric could still come over though, because he was a Communist too. We refused to say "under God" when we were pledging allegiance to the flag in school. Gene wouldn't sign a loyalty oath. Everyone was proud of him.

Eric and I formed a singing group called "The Minors." I mostly remember when we performed "Follow the Drinking Gourd" at the Songmakers Workshop Picnic and Hootenanny in Griffith Park. He played and sang and I did interpretive dance. People didn't usually beg us to perform.

My hometown was a time and place. It was long summers and easy school. It was a lot of freedom, and a family of five sharing one shower. It was having grandparents next door and a dog who could climb up a ladder onto the garage roof with me. It was Thrifty's calling, saying, "Could you please come and get your dog, she's sleeping in the doorway under the fan, and customers can't come into the store." It was the home that I couldn't wait to leave, that stays in my dreams when I feel like a stranger and people on Abbott Kinney Boulevard all use cell phones and look straight ahead.

2 CORINGA DRIVE

I wanted to be like one of the dancing girls in "Oklahoma" or "Seven Brides for Seven Brothers," with a lot of romantic drama, singing, dancing and twirly skirts, surrounded by shallow, brightly colored people and scenery. I would be Jane Powell or Shirley Jones. Later it was Natalie Wood or Rita Moreno (but that's when I started being Mexican).

I was Rita Moreno in " West Side Story" once, while I was drying the dishes, when my father bumped into me and I spat out in a perfect Puerto Rican accent, "DON'T YOU TOUCH ME!" I was really in trouble that time, but I just wanted to be dropped into one of those movies.

Coringa Drive wound up the side of the hill between Highland Park and Eagle Rock in Los Angeles. There were fields all around and lots of wildflowers. My dad would take me for "flower walks" to pick bouquets up the hill. He taught me the names of the flowers, and to leave as long a stem as possible when picking them. He said that by taking the flower, the plant grew stronger because more energy could go to the rest of it. He also taught me flower arranging, to put the taller flowers in the center, and spread out the colors so they would be balanced.

I spent a lot of my childhood in trees and on rooftops. Tangerine season would find me on top of the garage, not needing meals or company. I started out the season eating greenish tangerines, and kept eating them as they ripened. Plum season would find me down the hill a bit, deciding between sugar plums and the larger purple ones. There were apricots too, through the high grass. Loquats were between my grandma's house and the driveway, and pineapple guavas were in front of her house between her lawn and ours.

We also had twenty-nine avocado trees, grape vines, and an orange tree. There was sour grass to eat and honeysuckle to suck. There was a grapefruit tree that I sat in a lot, watching the ant trekkers, and not eating the nasty fruit. I can still feel the rough, dry maternal texture of her branches. They felt like my skin. My knees and feet were calloused and gray. I walked on gravel, and slid down cliffs. I'm still not comfortable with pavement.

Dad was an artist, a painter. His studio, which he built with my grandfather, served as the family room. There was an immense easel that faced the front door, which usually had a portrait on it, with somber colors and haunted eyes; or a landscape, with round, proletariat-looking people. The skylight leaked for the fifteen years we lived there. Garbage cans were placed around the room to catch the water in the rainy season, as Dad put tar endlessly around the glass. It never worked. I had a friend over once who just threw her peanut shells on the studio floor. I was offended, and my dad once was offended when an acquaintance came over and called our house "Tobacco Road," I guess after the novel or the film about sharecroppers in Georgia. I hadn't read the book, but I got the picture.

Birthdays were huge. There I'd be, in a frilly white dress with flowers my father pinned in my curly hair. Once again, I don't remember where my mother was. I see my dad's face, admiring and emotional. I always wanted to hide from that face; it was too much.

I really wanted the party to be normal for my school friends. My dad would perform for them "Ishcom Schpeil Conductor" and other participation songs in foreign languages, or with strange sounds. They never seemed normal or "Mouseketeer." My friends loved it. I wondered why they loved it so much, and why he had to be the boss of my birthday parties and get all the attention. There's one photo of Dad dragging me away to yell at me. I suppose it was a conflict over control.

We were an interesting bunch of kids . . . the children of the Communists, and the neighborhood kids of blue-collar families. The boys had rolled-up pant legs, sometimes one leg more rolled up than the other. The girls were in faded hard-to-iron cotton dresses with puffed sleeves. I was always darker than anyone else. I felt ugly—never clean, dry-skinned, hairy-legged, and knowing Beethoven from Schubert by the time I lost my front teeth. My brother's friend once said that I was a stick with a shock of hair and a look on my face like I had something to say to the world. Later I looked like I was trying too hard: posed. My dolls were all Anglo-Saxon Christians, with blonde or brown straight hair. They looked confident.

Grandpa and Grandma Wortis lived in a smaller house on the property with Aunt Ethel—Grandma's sister. My brother Alan lived in the second bedroom, downstairs, and later in the living room on a Murphy bed that we used for an amusement park ride, climbing up on top of it in the closet, then releasing it as it crashed to the floor. Dad eventually took it out and kept the closet for his art supplies, and Alan moved next door to Grandma and Grandpa's basement. The room was dingy, yet hip. I caught him kissing someone named Beverly there.

I got to move out of my parents' bedroom, because I was big. I wasn't the baby anymore who needed that bed with bars on one side. I was in a real bed—my brother Alan's bed, because he moved to the living room. I tried very hard not to mess it up. Two bookcases divided the space, half for Bob, and half for me. We shared the closet which had sliding doors. As we grew, Dad would add to the bookcases, creating a partition to separate us more. We still had to share the closet and the overhead light, though. When I had friends over we would keep Bob up and it pissed him off.

The other kids in the neighborhood weren't Jewish Communists like us, and they had sidewalks. We didn't, because we were in the hills. I wanted a sidewalk, like the other kids. The Christians could roller skate, and I couldn't. I had roller skates, but they were no good on the terraced land, or the steep, rough pavement of the driveway. The teacher once scolded us for not behaving like Christian boys and girls. Christians were like TV people, magazine people, dolls and classmates: normal people. They didn't sit in trees with hairy legs and scabby knees. They didn't have curly black hair and hand-me-downs.

My dad grew up in a neighborhood where everyone else seemed to celebrate Christmas. He'd walk through the snow and look through their windows, taking in the idyllic scenes, watching people singing around the Christmas tree and opening presents. Later, the kids would come out to play in the snow with new sleds and earmuffs. On Coringa Drive we had the biggest Christmas tree in the neighborhood. Easter was pretty spectacular, too, with three-quarters of an acre to hide Easter eggs. We spent our childhoods trying to help Dad make up for what he had missed.

I got my first new dress when I was eight. I needed one for the Easter Pageant at school. I happened to be at

Sears with a friend and saw a cute pink dress for $1.99. I had to open my big mouth and tell my mother about it. I realized how plain it was as soon as she got excited about the price, and tried to convince her that I needed something fancier for Easter. I didn't want to talk her out of the dress but I never meant for it to be my Easter dress. My mother bought it, and her friend, Florence, who taught high school crafts, covered the skirt with netting and put felt flowers around the waistband. I looked like a crafts project for the pageant. I hadn't developed a sense of humor about myself yet. Jane Powell would never have worn this.

3 COOKIE THE THIRD

When I was little I had a thing for parakeets. I loved their cages, their paraphernalia: the little bells, mirrors, plastic miniature toys. They had a little Disneyland life.

I named all of my parakeets Cookie. I set out to protect the first two Cookies from the outside world, but one of them died anyway and the other one flew away. The only thing worse than having a cage without a bird is having a cage with a bird that's dead. I saved up for Cookie Number One and Two with my own money, but my Aunt Helen said she'd buy me a parakeet if I cut off my hair.

My hair was a source of concern for the adults in my family. I had a lot of it. It was black, curly, and couldn't be tamed. My parents made me wear it in a ponytail—with very short bangs, or two ponytails, a look that made me resemble a small mouse—or cut off completely. I wanted long hair like the girl in the "before" part of the Toni Perm commercial. She'd come out with straight glossy hair, then she'd walk through a magic looking glass and emerge with her hair all curly. I felt like shouting, "Don't do it!" I wanted her *before* hair, but there was a new Cookie at the pet shop on Ave. 50 that needed rescuing.

Cookie the Third turned out to be a boy. That was why his nose was blue, but I didn't hold that against him. I just added Ray to his name. Except for the nose, he looked identical to the other Cookies—small and green—but Cookie Ray was even nicer. He became so tame that I could walk around the neighborhood with him on my shoulder. I talked to him, clipped his wings, cleaned his cage, and tried to teach him to talk. He never actually learned English, but I tried to understand him. I guess I tried harder to learn Parakeet.

One thing about him, though, was that he was afraid of my father. I felt proud that I was the only one for Cookie. My father was so powerful in so many ways, but I was best at winning the trust of one small bird.

One day I was standing in the kitchen with Cookie on my shoulder. My mother was frying bacon. My dad came up to me and put his finger out for Cookie to get on, and Cookie flew away, right into the pan of bacon. There he stood, lifting one foot, then the other. All sound was sucked out of the room, and all movement stopped, except for the lifting of the little feet. My mother must have turned off the stove, and my father must have picked up the bird from the pan. This must have happened, although I had stopped seeing.

My dad wrapped Cookie Ray in rags, and I brought him to Mrs. Rigney's house. Mrs. Rigney lived right behind us and had a room full of birds, many that she rescued. I hoped she could fix Cookie.

A few days later I went to pick up the same bundle, but this time it was dead. I didn't see him die. It was easier for me that way, but it wasn't fair. The bundle was put in a shoebox, and was buried down the hill, and there was some sort of ceremony. Or maybe that was when the rabbit who had maggots in his ear died, or maybe when the rooster died. Maybe it was the white rat. It's been over fifty years now and I still want to save him.

4 AUNT ETHEL

They used to say that Aunt Ethel had been a real beauty. It's not that I didn't believe them; it's just that to a kid, "real beauty" and "old lady" seemed out of place together. Especially since Aunt Ethel was stalk-thin and had a shock of frizzy white hair and lived next door at my grandparents' house in their dark, overcrowded second bedroom.

I would knock tentatively at Aunt Ethel's door and she would ask, "What do you want?" and I'd say, "Candy." I'd hear the bedsprings squeak, and the door creak open, and there she would be. She looked neither delighted nor annoyed to see me. She'd reach under her bed, past the boxes that mostly held scrapbooks and newspaper clippings, and bring out a tin of hard candy. I didn't particularly like the candy, but I'd unwrap the cellophane, and listen to her tell me about the clippings. Nothing she said seemed happy or interesting to me. I don't recall anyone else talking to her, and never heard of anything else she had left behind when she died.

Aunt Ethel had been jilted, so she never married. I never asked about this; I just asked what "jilted" meant. But I never asked for details—it was just who she was: a jilted candy provider next door. I imagined he must have been handsome and had money, kind of like the prince in Cinderella, but more Brooklyn style, because they came from Brooklyn.

My mother had a brother, Irving, who died at thirty. We never found out how, some kind of meningitis was suspected, but Grandma didn't want an autopsy. He had a copy of *Lust for Life* opened on his bedside table when they found him. My mother had a photo of Irving—he was very dashing, standing in front of a Model T with a girl on either side of him, both flappers, with their bobs, caps and reckless, gay attitudes. It all seemed right out of *The Great Gatsby*. I pictured Aunt Ethel's jilter like Irving.

Aunt Ethel was a Christian Scientist. I never asked about that, either, because my parents had a "don't go there" look about them when it was mentioned, so I figured it was a bad thing, and an embarrassment, because the rest of us were Jews and Atheists. Dick DeWitt's mother, they said, was a Christian Scientist, and when she got sick they didn't call a doctor, and she died. I had never met her, but I had a picture of her in my head, simply a skinny figure under a patchwork quilt, who was sick and then died. I was reassured by the fact that both Dick DeWitt and Aunt Ethel seemed fine.

Sometimes Aunt Ethel would leave for downtown in a taxi. It's the only time I'd seen a taxi, and it would wait for her up on the road, by the mailbox. When she returned she'd have a Golden Book for me, one of those skinny children's books they used to sell in the 50s: *Scuffy the Tugboat, The Pokey Little Puppy, Tootle.*

Aunt Ethel had a thing about dandelions. We lived on three-quarters of an acre with two large lawns, so there were plenty of dandelions to disturb her. She had special tools to dig out their roots, and she'd let me use one. I was admonished that if I didn't dig deep enough to get the root completely out that the whole dandelion would come back. This was a bad thing. All the digging, then, would have been for nothing. When the dandelion had a frizzy white head I was to sneak up on it, grab the entire head in my hand, then gouge out the root, while I had the seeds entrapped, not letting even one escape.

"Aunt Ethel died a Jew." There seemed to be some satisfaction in this. I don't remember anyone grieving, any funeral, or any fuss being made. It's that she used to be there, and then she wasn't. "She lived as a Christian Scientist, but she died a Jew." I guess they didn't get the whole root out, Aunt Ethel.

5 CHERRIES

When I was about eight I spent a week at Theresa's house. She was my mother's best friend. Only Diana, her daughter, and I were there. Butchy, Theresa's son, was outside. Thank God, because he could really be a pain. My brother told me that what I should do when Butchy went after me was to hit him real hard in the stomach, then when he doubled over, to give him a chop on the back of the neck and knee him in the gut. I did that once and I was amazed at how well it worked. Theresa got really mad at me, though. Butchy was crying and Theresa was comforting him and calling him "My Bubbela Boy." I felt bad that Theresa was mad at me, but I didn't feel bad that I gave it to Butchy.

Diana was a teenager and all that I aspired to be. She was beautiful and had a ponytail and straight hair. She was cool. People used to ask if we were sisters, but she would say, "No, cousins." But we really weren't cousins. Our mothers grew up together in the same neighborhood in Brooklyn. Even our grandparents knew each other. Diana told me I didn't have any cuticles. It's good to not have cuticles. I didn't know that then, but she also told me to wash my feet before I got into bed and that made me feel dirty. Her sheets were clean.

I was staying with the Kennedys because my parents were out of town. I walked into the living room, and Diana was sitting on the back of the couch eating something out of a bag. It didn't take me long to figure out that they were cherries and they looked like good ones. Bing.

Now cherries were and still are my favorite food, and Bing cherries—hard, crisp and juicy—could put me over the edge. And there was Diana, my almost-sister, with a bag entirely to herself. Theresa must have bought them for her. No one had ever bought cherries just for me. I wondered if they were just for her or if she was supposed to share them. She was eating them slowly, one-by-one, and I was hypnotized by the bulge in the bag, analyzing how many she had left. She took another one from the bag and ate it.

"Where's Theresa?"

"She left with my dad."

She rooted around for another and pulled it out by the stem. She looked at it as it dangled from her fingers, and then dropped it into her mouth and slowly began to chew. She ate another, looking at me. I watched mute, baffled, as one-by-one they disappeared. In my house they didn't do this. If someone had cherries, that person would have to share them. It just made sense that if I waited she would do the right thing and give me some. I didn't have words for Diana about this, because she had to do the right thing because she was great and she told everybody we were cousins.

The bag seemed to be getting pretty low, and so was my hope. Diana sure wasn't picking up my cues. I was using my survival skills. I was very pleasant and unobtrusive, just leaning into those cherries with my will.

Diana hung out with Cappy Israel and Jenny Vincent. Not the one from San Cristobal; the kid. And she was in the teenage group at Dance Center. They were amazing. They did this one dance about a bus stop, and Jenny was the bench. Everyone stepped on her, then looked at an imaginary watch. I had never seen anything that cool before. Kids couldn't have done that dance.

The bag rattled again and I averted my face like a Labrador Retriever and felt the cherries in my mind.

"Diana."

"What? Do you want one?" She ate another one.

She was still chewing. There were only about four left . . . now three. I thought Diana was like a sister to me. There were only two left.

"Do you want one?" she asked again.

"Yes."

I couldn't believe this. I would have shared them with her. And I was a pretty good dancer, too. She ate one more. There was only one left.

"Do you want it?"

"Yes." She bit it in half.

"Do you still want it?"

I was thinking. I didn't know the right answer.

"Yes."

She spat on it.

"Do you still want it?"

I wanted to be cruel to myself like she was being because I was not beautiful and proud and nobody bought me cherries.

"Yes." She handed it to me.

I took it into the kitchen and washed the spit off.

I ate that last half cherry.

6 APRIL FOOLS

My dad had a very sweet side. Child-like. My mother called him a noble soul, and she was married to him for sixty years. He used to try to communicate with birds. He would stand in the patio in his pajamas and purse his thin lips together and try to imitate their sound. He taught me how to talk to flowers. "Do you want a little water? Are you hungry? Do you want me to take that leaf off for you?" He also taught me how to arrange them. (This was all terrific modeling for when I was ready to find a life partner: You don't talk to flowers? What kind of a man are you? But that's another story).

He had grown up with three brothers and no sisters, and went to an all-boys school. I was the third child, and the only girl. He wasn't crazy about his mother (she was artistic and temperamental), but he told me a lot about his Aunt Sarah, who never spoke above a whisper. He liked her a lot. This was the sum total of his experience with women.

He was telling me one day about how there would be peace and harmony all over the world after the revolution came. He painted a very beautiful oil painting of the lion lying down with the lamb. He even wrote a song about it. I asked him how the lion would eat. He thought for a while and told me that science would find some sort of plant protein for lions, maybe. I was and still am skeptical. I didn't tell him, however. You don't want to burst that bubble.

The bubble, while it was in full effect, did make my father the perfect target for April Fool's Day. I remember picking blossoms from a neighbor's hydrangea bush and tying it to ours. Ours would never bloom, so when Dad saw it he was so thrilled, but when he found out what I'd done he crashed—and when he crashed he held on to his grudge forever. When I was ten I tried (with a saleslady) to get him to buy me two dresses instead of one. When I was thirty he threw it back at me as an example of my betrayal and greed.

April Fool's Day was so cute in school. That's where I learned about it—salt in the sugar bowl and sugar in the saltshaker . . . there's a spider on your back, and all that. I wanted so much to be a typical normal American girl who did things like that, so I tried it: salt in the sugar bowl and sugar in the salt shaker, and I sat in wait on the bench of the nasty 1911 black baby grand piano that dominated the living room.

My dad entered, in his bubble. His eyes were vacant. This was perfect. I saw him enter the kitchen and get a coffee cup. Yes. I heard the sound of it filling with coffee. I held my breath. Through the open door I saw him go to the sugar bowl and put one, two (yes!), three heaping teaspoons of the contents of the sugar bowl in his coffee. He put the cup absently to his lips, and with a faraway look on his face began to drink. He was really slugging it down, focused (as usual) on something in the distance, something noble; perhaps the lyrics to a new song, perhaps a touchup on one of his paintings, perhaps a poem.

When the coffee finally registered, his face turned green, then purple, and he went running. I heard the coffee spraying into the sink. Mission accomplished.

But it didn't feel like I thought it would, and I fell from grace, once again. There were no more Aunt Sarahs. I was Jezebel. I was the traitor. I was Goneril in King Lear. I was my brother's ex-wife when she left. I was the third child, the accident, who took him away from his painting. I was the Bourgeoisie.

My dad's been gone for more than 25 years now. Look who's standing in the patio in my pajamas trying to communicate with the crow on the power line? The crow thinks I'm an asshole. He's had it with humans. He wants me to go in the house and watch TV where I won't bother anybody. I go up the stairs past the withering philodendron. It was dying, but I didn't have the heart to throw it in the trash.

7 MOM

When I was a girl I had skin as white as snow, cheeks as red as two red apples, and jet black hair with just a slight wave. I was the curly-haired one of the family. People would stop my mother on the streets and tell her it wasn't right for a child to wear makeup. My mother told me these words, over and over when I was growing up. I was also led to believe that I was no great beauty, and was talented, but lazy and disorganized.

My mother said she was going to write a book on the raising and feeding of geniuses. I knew this included my father and my brothers, but suspected it didn't include me. I was encouraged to take typing, cooking, and sewing. I didn't want to raise and feed geniuses—I wanted to be one. So I did what I felt was necessary, cultivating eccentricities like going without shoes and wearing earrings made out of old eyeglass nosepieces, left over from my grandfather's optical store. There seemed to be a missing piece to this genius business, though, and I wasn't able to get a handle on it—at least not in my mother's eyes.

Mom graduated high school at fifteen, getting the highest score in the state of New York in the French part of the Regency Exam. I struggled to get out of high school because I hated it, so I took extra classes and talked the school psychologist into promoting me early. I didn't get the highest score in anything but I made it out by sixteen, just barely.

Mom hummed when she got pissed off. The hum had no recognizable melody. It seemed self-righteous at the time, but on reflection it might have been the type of hum I make when someone is getting murdered in a movie in an unusually graphic and painful way, and I close my eyes and hum to blot out the horrible death cries. When mom got pissed off it usually was at me. I wanted her approval, but got it only sporadically. I couldn't trust it. When she asked to see my Master's thesis, a two-act play, her comments upon finishing it were, "You have a good ear for dialogue," and "Has your shrink seen this?" The approval was met with a swift counter. I didn't have much time to bask in it. On another occasion she told me that Mary Hiddleman, her friend, said that I'd look just like Elizabeth Taylor if I only lost weight. These compliments didn't go to my head.

When I was in a dance recital at school, my friends and I did a number we named, "Three Blind Rats," to the score of Fellini's "8 ½." We each represented a vice: I was

Prejudice, Lisa was Greed, and Rosemary was Vanity. The teacher didn't want us to perform it. She wanted something lighter, but the class insisted that we be included in the show. I don't remember any praise, though. I just remember, "You know you were the fattest one on stage" and "Bonnie Frieden has such good carriage", and my father's "Who was that beautiful Oriental girl?"

When my dad died I wrote a piece about him. My mother read it to my uncles and said, "They had to leave the room, they were so upset." I thought it was a tribute to my father. I didn't mean to upset anyone.

Growing up I felt that I was carrying the Karma of someone who had done the unspeakable, and never could be forgiven. I don't know what that unspeakable was, but I honored it, and assumed responsibility for it.

I loved this woman, my mother, with her sharp wit, sense of humor, and beauty. But I didn't want to be like her. If growing up meant I had to occupy her space, I wanted no part of it. My brother Alan sent me to a psychiatrist when I turned eighteen. I was afraid to go. I was afraid of confronting the monster that I thought I must be and had concealed from myself. When my psychiatrist said after two years, "You're not so bad," I cried all the way home. Alan asked me what I had learned in psychoanalysis. I told him I learned that he was my mother figure. Alan said, "I want my money back."

When I read *East of Eden,* I saw my mother in Cathy Ames and was appalled by my seeing her that way. What was wrong with me?

Mom was kind to animals, loved our dogs, but was cold to me. My tears got no sympathy. They just seemed to annoy her. My father, who wasn't any more comfortable with my emotions, sang to me, a form of good-natured ridicule,

"Don't cry my little girl.
Come and just sit down beside me.
Wait till recess is over
I'll see what they've done to thee…"

all the while looking to see who was watching his performance, like others were in on it. I became a bathroom crier.

I wasn't unhappy as a child. My grandparents doted on me, and I was the darling of several teachers. I did feel apologetic sometimes, just for being me, for occupying space when I was at home. I acted out. I stole sunglasses from Thrifty Drug Store. I stole clothes from Bullochs Departmant Stores. I joined book clubs and record clubs and didn't pay. I didn't clean my room. Not ever.

When Mom died I had moved about an hour away. I went to Kaiser Permanente on Sunset Blvd. and they handed me her shoes and her purse. I didn't want to see her, but my daughter, Hannah, who was about fourteen at the time, did. She needed that completion. My other daughter, Rosie, who was about ten at the time, slept with my mother's shoes, and a wig she bought in case she lost her hair during chemotherapy. As far as I know she still has them.

Mom's ashes were interred under the yellow roses at Pierce Bros. Westwood Village Memorial Park "where the stars are buried," right near Marilyn Monroe. We bought a brass plaque for her at the cemetery and hung it on the rose bushes, but it disappeared. We bought another one to stick in a concrete display nearby. I arranged the memorial service, wearing her slip and underwear. The minister said she was wearing her mother's slip, and her mother had died seven years before.

Now, all I have is a dwindling supply of jewelry. I gave almost all of it to my daughters. I still have a soup ladle, a frying pan, a gold pin, and one silver earring.

Sometimes I hear her when I talk to my daughters:

"Where did you get *that* dress?"

She also shows up when I get snippy with my husband: sarcastic, cynical.

Young women of my mother's era screamed when they saw Frank Sinatra. My mom screamed when she saw Buddy Ebsen. She loved loose-limbed dancing, and he was the loosest. Seventy years later she was still embarrassed by the display of silly emotion.

She loved that Perry Como was so relaxed. She loved Bob Newhart, Bob Crane, and anyone with good carriage. She loved people who were "quick on the draw." I tried to drill Anthony, my second husband, to be "quick" when he met her.

"And what do *you do*?" I drilled him.

"Watermelon," he shot back.

It was the first thing that came to his mind.

When I started trying to heal I brought back an exercise from Co-Counseling, a form of therapy I had been studying. I had Mom say twenty things she liked about my father.

"He's honest, he's a noble soul, he's a talented painter…"

Then I asked her to name twenty things she liked about herself. The only thing she said was,

"I put up with him for all these years."

She collapsed in laughter and that ended our session.

I know she wanted to be close to me. I wanted to be close to her. Her barbs prevented me. I couldn't get past them. Sometimes I think that her anger towards me was a sign of love; that she thought so highly of me I couldn't live into her image of me. I guess I'll never know. I want my daughters to be healthy, happy, and nice to me. That's it.

When my mom died I felt that I'd have the rest of my life to unravel our relationship, that there would be no new material to muck up the works. How naïve I was. I'm still just as lost as I was the day she died. I'm not closer to understanding. I still want her approval.

8 THE GIFT

My oldest brother has always been a trendsetter for our family. He started all of us on the Bossa Nova in the '60s. I remember the day he turned us all on to João Gilberto. Alan bought my dad his first car when he was only 16 (Alan, not my dad). He turned us on to Freud, again in the '60s, then meditation in the '70s. His guidance was always respected. Sometimes revered. The name Alan was spoken in italics, as in "*Álan* said" or "*Álan* does it this way." I spent many years hating Alan for this, but try as I might, I never mastered not respecting him.

I was fifteen the day he bought my parents a hand-held back massager. My mother took it out of the box and passed it around like some relic from an Egyptian museum. We found it had a switch, and it started vibrating with a gentle hum when the switch was turned on. We were a gifted family. We discovered very soon what it was for: massaging the upper back, which would magically make my mother belch, loud and long. She called it "grepz." I still don't know if it was a legitimate Yiddish word or a family word. I've embarrassed myself in the past not knowing the difference. Anyway, I never figured out how she could do that, just from the upper back being stimulated; but there you were.

When my friends came over I would treat them to a buzz. I was the only one in my crowd who had one. We tried it everywhere. Vibrating the top of the head was bizarre. It made a rattling sound. The cheek made the nose vibrate until you sneezed. It made singing so great when you put it on your chest and sang.

I grew up in an artistic family, so exploration was expected, and ignored, unless you took my father's brushes and didn't put them back. If you did something like that he would stomp around the house, head thrust forward, fists clenched, saying, "Kids and dogs, boy; kids and dogs . . . " or any of several of his favorite sayings.

It was great on the ear, and on the soles of the feet. My parents kept it in the dining room, on the imitation Swedish chest where the music books were stored. I don't remember the day I first tried sitting on it, but I was a bright kid, a creative kid, and I was fifteen when we bought the house with the music book chest, and seventeen when I moved out for the first time, so it was somewhere in there. Sit on it I did. And from then until I left home, each time my parents left the house I was sitting on it.

I began suspecting something was wrong with me, because it seemed totally out of my control. I couldn't not do it. I loved it more than any plaything I had ever had. I couldn't wait for my parents to leave the house. I'd move it to the living room and watch TV in ecstasy. I didn't care what I watched anymore.

By the time I was eighteen, *Alan* decided to send me and my brother to see a shrink. My mother said it was because I was afraid of men. But that's another story. I was certainly afraid of the shrink they picked out.

I vomited and staggered around with a migraine the entire day I was supposed to go. It took me a year to recover from the initial visit. The shrink looked like an undertaker. When he put his hand on my shoulder I jumped. His voice was balmy and syrupy-sympathetic. I refused to go back. Finally, my brother Bob's shrink recommended someone for me. It took me about a year of working with him for me to confess what I had been up to. I think I was expecting him to send me for shock therapy, or penance, or maybe even jail. But he didn't. He shook his head and knitted his bushy brows and said in his Czechoslovakian accent, "Oh, everybody does it."

I still find that hard to believe.

9 ANNETTE

"Oh, Bonnie, you always use such big words!" I had tried so hard to be like the other kids, but I slipped up, using the word "vague" in the hash line, the line we used at recess to buy crap, instead of the crap that they sold in the cafeteria. I couldn't wait to get out of there. Then we moved to Silverlake, where I thought I might be able to use a word like "vague" and not get singled out. I was excited about starting a new school. And finally, there I was, at Marshall High School, with its good ratings: overweight, broken out, and wearing my mother's underpants.

Annette was in my second period. Spanish 2B. She was different from the other kids in the mid-60s. She wore a gray jumper and a hand-knit cardigan instead of a mini-skirt. Instead of wearing her hair in a flip she had it pulled half up and half down with bangs. Her hair was very dark and her skin was really light. She didn't use black eyeliner, either, or any makeup for that matter.

Annette and I walked home the same way, although we tried to pretend we didn't know each other. One day I was walking half a block in front of her for several blocks, and decided to be brave and acknowledge her presence. So I waited for her at the corner, to her obvious annoyance.

I said hello, and so did she, although my voice always sounded like I was eight, and she had a beautiful, adult-sounding voice. I thought she sounded like she had a slightly phony accent, as if she were in a Shakespearean play. I thought it was wonderful.

"I didn't know you lived this way," I said, casually.

"Yes, we've been living here for years."

"We just moved here. We were living in Highland Park. I couldn't stand it anymore. It was so provincial."

"I don't know Highland Park." Annette looked up the street, towards where she turned off.

"You haven't missed much."

We walked in silence for a few minutes.

"Well, I turn off here," she said, looking relieved.

"Are you walking tomorrow?" I asked, amazed by my brashness.

"Yes, but I'm going to be late. I have rehearsal."

"What are you rehearsing for?" I asked, shifting my books to my other hip.

"A play. 'Curious Savage.'"

"Really? I act too!"

"What kind of acting do you do?" she asked, trying to appear polite.

"Well, I'm studying method acting, but I've only been in plays at school, and at The University of Judaism."

"Is that what you want to do?"

"Yes."

"Well, I plan to be a Broadway actress." She knit her brows and put her books down on the sidewalk, buttoning her cardigan.

"Really? My brother's starring on Broadway!"

I didn't find out until much later that she thought I was totally full of shit.

I went to see Annette in "Curious Savage" and thought she was brilliant. She played an older woman with a Shakespearean accent. I had been struggling through a copy of *An Actor Prepares* that my brother had sent me, and had read any play I could get my hands on, so from my taxed fifteen-year-old brain I had found a soul mate.

We started hanging out. I had the use of my mother's '54 Ford, which was fine as long as we hung our heads out the window when we were driving. The exhaust fumes were really intense. You could even see them sometimes billowing out from under the dashboard. Maybe Mom had a delayed subconscious euthanasia wish. When we could get together a dollar for gas, we'd go to Jessup's Dairy in Glendale to look at the cows.

"Look at those babies! My God, look at those lashes! I want one!" I did want a cow.

"Those pregnant cows are enormous! Poor things. It's bad enough to be pregnant. But to be pregnant and a cow!"

"Look at the size of that one! Jesus! Look at those udders!"

"Those aren't udders, you idiot! That's a bull!"

"Oh, God."

We got free milk sometimes. Now that was an over-the-top experience for teenagers.

Sometimes we hung out at Pickwick Bookstore in Hollywood. If I had money I'd share (Annette's parents were even tighter than mine. I don't think she'd even seen money, except for the twenty cents they'd give her for lunch, which she used to buy two candy bars with, which I thought was brilliant. She weighed 110 pounds, and I thought that maybe that was the secret. It didn't work for me, though).

We each had an apple crate that we kept in our rooms at home. We'd line the books up as we read them. Maybe she didn't know it, but I would go nuts if her row got longer than mine, or if someone moved a book out of the Bonnie Decimal System.

We had a lot in common, but we were different in a few ways. I was needy. I acted out, ate too much, ran around at night and shoplifted. I'd steal things like traffic cones, and hairbrushes at Thrifty's. Things like traffic cones were a form of pop art to me, although I couldn't articulate it then. I took brushes, sunglasses, and other paraphernalia because I needed them and didn't have any money.

My mother used to say, "Bonnie could wear out three friends in a day." Annette didn't act needy. She could stay in her room for days and draw, paint, or make potholders on little looms and sew them together. She was self-sufficient. And she was thin. Even though her background was as fucked up as mine, she didn't stuff her feelings with food, like I did.

I finished high school early, then Annette graduated and went off to college. Driving from Silverlake to Northridge felt like a trek across Africa.

One day I got a letter from Annette. I waited until I was on the bus to read it, because I was late for my shrink's appointment, and the two-hour bus ride could use all the help it could get.

I was in love with Larry Richardson and Howard Cooper, and their letters gave me a rush, but my best friend's letters kept me going.

I got on the bus at Vermont and opened the letter. Annette sounded like she was thinking of suicide. She didn't feel that she had anything to live for. My breathing stopped. I felt a blow to the solar plexus. The bus stopped. The door opened in front of The Braille Institute and a woman got on. She was black (I was just staring now) but she didn't have a face. She was wearing dark sunglasses. There was no nose, just two little nostrils. All the rest was featureless scar tissue. There was just a gash where her mouth should be, but the gash was smiling, and she was chattering cheerfully with her helper and the people on the bus as she boarded. I looked down at Annette's letter in my lap and I felt sick.

Damn you, Annette. Don't you dare, Goddamn it!

I groped in my purse for a pen and tore some paper out of the notebook I kept for writing poetry. I started writing a letter to Annette. All I kept thinking was, "Don't you Goddamn dare!" I told her about the woman on the bus.

I told Annette I wanted to be like her—beautiful, interesting, and thin. I wanted to be able to focus on art projects for hours. I wanted a deeper voice, with more integrity, more authority. I wanted to be less needy. I wanted an internal life that kept me entertained.

"I wanted to be you, Annette. You don't say this. You don't think this and you don't do this. Don't you ever."

I realize now that I had a similar feeling when my eight-year-old daughter got hit by a car, and I was waiting in the lobby of U.S.C. Medical Center for the results. There was a fierceness that I felt.

They WOULD (both for Annette and my daughter, Rosie) live and they WOULD be fine, and they were. It didn't feel like it was my personal will. The rage felt transcendent; defiant. It was a power I don't understand. I certainly don't own it, play with it, or use it normally. I just remember it, and it scares me.

I mailed the letter when I transferred at Wilshire. I got a call from Annette a few days later. When she got my letter she put her fist through a window.

Annette and I had dinner last Thursday. She told me that she hadn't put her fist through the window because of my letter. She's still thin. She looks good. She's much more down to earth than she used to be. She's an artist and a landscape gardener. She's still my inspiration in many ways. She has a flare for things, and her speaking sounds authentic to me. She still stays home mostly. I'm still acting out.

10 CAMP

I'm here as a lie. I'm living a lie. If they find out, I'm doomed. I am the one who's supposed to be so full of truth. I'm full of it, all right. I just want to go home. Now. I never wanted to be Jewish. I'm a Marxist. I hate all this Jewish crap. What am I doing here with rabbis? Miriam and her ideas.

Bonnie, I really think it's time you had a Jewish education. You are Jewish, you know.

I hate my roommates. Little Westside bitches. One of them keeps plucking her armpits with tweezers. Little nose job fashion plate sheltered little bitches. I don't need this shit. I want to go home! I've lived in New York on welfare corn grits. I lived with a thirty-year-old man and smoked pot and studied *The Tibetan Book of the Dead* and I need this shit? I don't belong here.

Dear Mother Come and Fetch me.

Dear Mother take me home.
I'm drunk and unhappy
And my virginity's gone.

Today I stayed in bed. I told them I had the flu, but they dragged me out because they *didn't want me to miss the 10:00 lecture.* Fuck the lecture. I don't want to know. I'm a tormented Bohemian artist. Next time I'll try hiding on the roof.

\#

Peter Mandell caught me in the kitchen with one hand full of stewed prunes and an ice cream bar in the other. Like a genius I hide under the table. Someone had talked about midnight raids on the kitchen and I thought it would be cool. It wasn't. I am so humiliated. I feel like such an asshole. I want to go home.

\#

Actually, I hate to admit it, but that last lecture was pretty good. I don't remember exactly what the rabbi said, but it made sense to me. I felt a little opening. I'm not a convert or anything, but I didn't hate that lecture as much as I thought I would. I always thought there was a fixed idea of what God was, so I had no trouble being an atheist. If I don't know what God is, then being an atheist would just be rebelling against what I don't understand. I like to know what I'm rebelling against. If I ease up on my definition of God, can I include God in my belief system?

So I am walking back to the bunk on the path through the woods. It's 10:00 at night. Sharon is following me. She thinks I'm wonderful for some reason. She's this mousy little thing. I'm looking at the sky and I'm thinking, "Could there really be a God? Could I have been wrong for nineteen years? Wouldn't it be amazing if what I was so sure of wasn't real, and what I was wasn't?" So I say out loud, for Sharon's benefit as well as mine, "Okay, God. If you exist show me a sign, because I'm ready, God. I want to know."

As soon as I finished talking the ground started to rumble and the hills around started to blaze. Sharon fell to the ground on her knees and started to cry,

"You're a saint! You're a saint!" she sobbed.

My jaw dropped and I started to shake. My bones were vibrating and so was my mind. I don't know how long it took to stop, or for us to move.

"Rockadyne."

"What?"

"Stop crying, Sharon, it was Rockadyne. They must have launched a missile."

#

Many people would have been transformed by this experience, would have become devout, maybe turning towards altruism, or maybe even martyrdom. Me, I spoke briefly to Peter about joining the Freedom Riders, going to the South and laying my life on the line for integration. Peter suggested that I might make a larger impact through my acting or writing. So I agreed, although nothing much came of it.

All my life there has been a community that welcomed me, that called me one of their own, despite the fact that I have pulled my roots to the snapping point. This community is as foreign to me as the Amish, or the Inuit. The culture baffles me as much as any culture, yet all my life this community has beckoned me to "come home." I have not "gone home," and the shift in me was subtle. Perhaps there was a chink that opened that day, a chink for some of the infinite to shine through. But the ground did tremble and the hills did blaze, and I did hear a distant rumble.

#

"I believe in the coming of the Messiah, although he may delay. I still believe." I'll never know what that was all about, but something opened in me that never completely closed.

#

Grandma, I want very much to name my daughter after you, but not out of custom or duty. Out of love.

#

When I got home I bought a loaf of challah and made my parents watch while I lit the candles. They rolled their eyes. Did you know that in Hebrew "creation" and "suffering" have the same root? I think I've found myself. I am going to make a difference. I am going to be an actress. I am going to keep the traditions alive.

ROBERTSON

We Fought Till Our Hands Were Meat

We fought till our hands were meat
And he humiliated my dress
My rage froze
As I watched him self-destruct

Later, from the trampled floor
Under a cast-off lamp
I held his pieces in my lap
And slept
For him to become whole again

11 TIM

I remember you coming into the room, noticing me, and sitting down near the front.

"Voice and Diction." The teacher was extremely effeminate and theatrical, whose aunt unfortunately was Tallulah Bankhead. I say "unfortunately" because he often threw "Aunt Tallulah" references at us to impress us, as in "Aunt Tellulah used to say…"

I remember noticing you. Nice. Comfortable.

We had to do a scene together from *The Importance of Being Earnest* and then you helped me with my Scottish accent. I couldn't get it right, and your grandfather was Scottish, and you had lived in Edinburgh for a year, so you were a professional.

We met in the student cafeteria to talk about homework, and I ran into someone I knew. I apologized to him because I "had to go meet this guy from my class" and I was a little embarrassed about you. I played both sides and apologized to you, and when I introduced you to my other friend you shouted out "Peter!" and he shouted out "Tim!" and you threw your arms around each other. It's odd, but that exact scenario happened again after we had separated, with you and a different friend of mine, except I was more apologetic the second time.

I invited you to my 21st birthday party. You looked nice and played the guitar, and Sue Hollis, who was staying with me, teased me that I liked you. I thought it was curious that she thought so. You were my friend. We went to the beach together, and you put your hand on my shoulder like I was one of your football buddies. I liked that. I had other guy friends that summer: Sam Rotter, who played "The Captain" in *Oh Dad Poor Dad,* and Patrick Lindley, who took me backstage to listen to him play the harpsichord. I remember throwing the most off-the-wall suggestions at him like "Alexander Nevski" and he'd be able to play them.

I had a ten-minute monologue in *Oh Dad Poor Dad,* and you came over to help me with my lines (I was living in the guest-house behind my parents' house).

We were in back of the house, sitting under the loquat tree. Sam appeared from around the corner with a shocked look on his face. You said, "Hello, Sam" and I said, "We were working on my lines." It occurred to me then that I was on your lap and you had your hand up my pants. Sam left. You carried me into the guesthouse and threw me on my bed. I said, "I'm not using anything." And you asked, "What about the future?"

After that we found it impossible to separate physically for more than a few hours at a time.

My nephews came over with my brother's ex-wife when you were at your father's, and I was so tense that day from all the people and all the drama that Annette, my best friend, gave me one of her brother's Stelazines (a tranquilizer). It didn't work, so she gave me another the next day. I went for a walk, and my head kept turning to the left. It was such a curious thing, and I couldn't seem to stop it. I kept arguing with myself, but my head, as if independently from the rest of me, kept looking left. It kept getting worse. When I got home I had to get into bed. You came over, and someone called my shrink and he prescribed something. You drove me to Thrifty's on Vermont, and left me in the car while you went inside to fill the prescription. I was there in the parking lot, sitting in your 1960 light-blue VW Bug, basically drooling over my left shoulder. A young black man in a crisp suit came to the window, holding a stack of "Mohammad Speaks." He saw me and asked if I was aware of the teaching of our prophet Elijah Mohammed. Then he looked a bit closer and said, "Oh, baby," then asked, "did you take something bad?" I nodded, mostly to the left, tongue lolling, and he told me to go to Orange Julius, get a Julius, and tell them to break a couple of raw eggs into it, and that would straighten me right out.

You got back with the prescription, and I took it right away. It didn't take long for it to take effect, and you stayed with me until you were sure I was okay. That was a hell of a date.

I remember another occasion when my mother said or did something to upset me and you picked me up in your car and stroked my head as I cried into your lap.

You didn't know if you would still want me when you became a rock and roll star, and that offended me. I went home to my mother's. Two days later you proposed, handing me the biggest bouquet of flowers I had ever seen. You told me that you would have gotten me a puppy but didn't have enough time. We got married about a week later.

It was 1969, and there were plenty of drugs. Drugs fascinated you, and you were into experimenting. You said you wanted to try heroin, just once one day. That scared me. But that wasn't the deal breaker. When I got pregnant and you wanted me to get an abortion I couldn't stay. Our daughter was going to be named Rebecca. She was going to have dark braids and run down grassy hills with her brother, Rannoch.

When you get divorced you lose a lot of music. You got The Byrds, The Stones, Bob Dylan and all the blues. I never wanted to hear BB King, Eric Clapton, Taj Mahal, any of them again.

Many years later you came to see me. You wanted my forgiveness. We sat up all night talking, and smoked a joint. I felt like I was with my best friend—like I had come home. In the early morning you tried to kiss me, and I knew I was not home. I told you I couldn't do it to your wife, which maybe was partly true. I couldn't do it to anybody, especially me.

That fall I woke up one morning at five a.m. gripping the blankets. I had dreamt that my mother was dying and I was screaming in the hospital for someone to do something. Her heart had stopped and I couldn't make anyone come help. Hours later when I had finally gotten back to sleep, the phone rang, waking me up again. It was your mother whom I hadn't spoken to in more than fifteen years, saying you'd died that morning. It was your heart.

Before the funeral I had another dream that woke me up. A glass skeleton was chasing me and her index finger was a lethal injection. Days later your ex-girlfriend, whom I'd met at the funeral, told me you died with a needle in your arm.

Now my daughter's got her own blues band. She'd blow your mind, Tim. It was crazy going from show to show. She got married on stage at "The Gig," put down her bouquet, picked up an electric guitar and belted. Her husband makes faces like Bill Burleigh when he plays lead guitar. It's crazy being at their house and hearing all your old favorites. I could name some of them for you, but you'd have more fun doing it yourself. You used to bounce around on your toes and get all puffed up when you were name-dropping with other people who knew the blues.

I stopped seeing a shrink when we got married. I stopped acting, too. Nothing could compete with the full body rush of you calling me pretty as I opened my eyes in the morning. I don't regret it, Tim. If we had been older, or known better, it wouldn't have been so painful, or so beautiful. I'm glad I'm older now, but someone said when you cast out the devils, you cast out the angels as well. I wish I could have kept a piece of what we had with me.

You told me a story once, Tim, about a guy who was shipwrecked on an island and lived there alone for many years, and one day a beautiful young girl also shipwrecked and landed on the same small island, and because you were the son of a Baptist preacher, of course she had her way with him. Later she asked him what he thought of the experience and he said, "It was great, but it sure took the spring out of my pebble flipper."

That's what you did, Tim. You took the spring out of my pebble flipper.

12 HAPPY NEW YEAR

I was living in Long Beach in a huge house with many other people. It was New Year's Eve, 1970. Tim's best friend, Jon; his wife, Sandy; and their German shepherd, Lady; were living with us. Tim, Jon, and Sandy had all been raised fundamentalist Christians, not that that had anything to do with how that New Year's turned out, but maybe it did.

A sociology student who looked like a geek lived in one of the bedrooms upstairs. He had short hair parted on the side and black glasses, and worked at Ralph's. His girlfriend would come on the weekends, showing up with a little, square overnight case. She had mousy brown hair and also wore glasses. Late at night we would hear the iron bed squeak, followed by her agonized moaning which built to bloodcurdling screams. Then it would be quiet. It kept us up, but we never said anything. At the end of the weekend they would leave together with her little Samsonite case. They never spoke to us.

This strange poet lived over the garage. We'd have to climb a ladder to visit him. Once he borrowed a book of children's poetry that my mother had given me. Her friend Dolly's granddaughter had a poem in it that she had written when she was five. He gave it back to me all marked up. I felt violated.

That weekend I had my thirteen-year-old nephew and Dolly's nineteen-year-old granddaughter with me. I guess Mom and Dolly hoped I might be a stabling influence on the kids. After all, I was happily married, and a college student. Maybe they just wanted to get rid of them.

We decided to have a party so I made a transparent mini dress (with a flesh-colored body suit under it). I looked very cute.

People started arriving and the party started taking off. The music was loud and the Boone's Farm was flowing. Suddenly, Sandy came running into the living room, screaming. Lady had gone into labor, had a stillborn puppy, and ate it, all except for the head. Sandy kept running in and out of the back room, checking on Lady, shrieking each time after finding an additional head or limb. Jon had disappeared. Somebody finally found him. He was upstairs screwing Dolly's granddaughter.

Tim took mescaline and I was furious at him. How could he have done something so huge without even consulting me? Why didn't he offer me any? He was acting weird, all blue-space-eyed and childlike. We argued, then started grabbing at each other until it escalated into a hands-on fight and he tore my dress. I didn't know what to do with all my anger, so I took some mescaline for revenge. I began to feel like a child, then a cartoon, then an Aubrey Beardsley drawing. When I pinned my dress together again and had gone back into the living room, the floor was covered with drunk people I didn't know. Things just kept getting weirder. Just after midnight the doorbell rang and Sandy (who was a mess) went to answer it.

Standing at the door was a pretty woman in a cocktail dress holding a martini in one hand. She said, "Is Jon here?" Sandy became hysterical.

Adam (my nephew) and I went to Cherry Park (on the corner) to air out. Things were looking like a cartoon to me, as people started entering the park from all four corners, carrying bongos, congas, and other percussion instruments (as if on cue) and gathered at the stage in the park. One conga player had brought his five-year-old sister whom he was supposed to be babysitting. She took me to the playground and led me through all of the equipment there. We went on the merry-go-round, the slide, and the swings. She was wearing a sparkly Christmas ornament in her hair like a fairy; she reminded me of a woodsy, magical creature, almost unbearably beautiful. The drums stopped, and my friend's brother reappeared to take her home. She looked at me and carefully took the ornament out of her hair. She handed it to me and they walked together toward the corner of the park and disappeared.

CASTELLUCCIO

Liberty Enlightening the World

You are a woman
Whose arm hasn't faltered for a hundred years.
You are so right. We are safe
Behind you. Mama, hide me in your robes.
Keep them back with your torch. Keep them from
Landing with your spiked
Crest. Pummel them with your slab. Mama,
It feels like I swallowed bottle caps.
This city has sharp nails, Mama. There
Are blinking eyes in the sky and they
Snarl softly at night and circle my
Bed. The bay sucks at your feet.

Thick-waisted hermaphrodite, Shield me
From the world.
Keep the bullies out

13 ANTHONY

It took me eight years to get my BA. I took many courses such as "Cinema Dramatic Art" and "Reevaluation Education" and six undergraduate courses in poetry. I usually got A's in those, which offset the C courses, like political science and astronomy and my D in geology. My grade average, actually, was high enough to get me into the Honors Program in English where I could take whatever I wanted as long as I took a few *pro-seminars* in courses like *The Satirical Novel* and *The Contemporary Novel*. I actually found a way to write the same paper for both, using John Updike's *Bech, A Book*, which was a contemporary satirical novel. I went to five different schools to gather credits, and dropped out between schools. Anything had to be better than the torture of listening for hours on a hard seat.

I don't remember if my mother actually bought me a one-way ticket to New York for a graduation present, or the hundred dollars that I used to buy the ticket. L.A. was closing in on me. New York was magical, exciting.

My brother picked me up at the airport, and brought me to his home in Connecticut. His family were all actors, and they didn't know that I was actually a highly acknowledged and successful actress who just killed in Cal State L.A.'s production of *Marat-Sade*. I played Rossignol, and for those of you who haven't been in *Marat-Sade*, Rossignol was one of the crazy people in clown face. Actually she was the only woman clown, the diva clown, who did the singing and dancing.

I had worked with the doctor at Cal State L.A., who put me on a diet and gave me diet pills. I was weighing in at 115 pounds. My dreams had come true for myself. I was a thin singer, dancer, and actress; highly acclaimed, and a graduate.

Unfortunately, the rest of Connecticut wasn't aware of my diva status, and the house guests and the rest of the family had triumphs that seemed a bit more triumphant, and they were casual about them. So I planted myself in the kitchen for ten days where the Pepperidge Farm cookies lived, gained back the ten pounds, and asked to be dropped off in The Village with Suzie.

Suzie, a friend of the family, was a few years older and had been a bad influence on me since I was fourteen, when she took me to get my ears pierced. She felt like my cousin. I would go stay with Suzie in New York whenever Los Angeles would become too painful. They say you always take yourself with you. Whenever I took myself to New York I felt surrounded by "my people" who "got" me. In L.A. I was more of a freak and I don't mean that in '60s jargon. I could read when I was two, read Dostoyevsky by 16, was off-the-wall, and couldn't bear to wear shoes.

When I arrived in The Village I bumped into Johnny Gonzales on the street. He had come to my 14th birthday party in Highland Park and went to Cathedral High, where all the cute guys went. He was living on the street so I took him up to Suzie's and fed him. When she got home she had a fit and told me I wasn't to bring any more men up to her place. I wasn't to give out her phone number, either. Did I understand?

My friend Jane, whom I worked with at Barnes & Noble, came over one night. We found Johnny and went folk dancing on 14th Street. I was obsessed with folk dancing, and, hey, it was free.

So there Anthony was, with his friend Vinny Devingo. Anthony looked so familiar, like my dad's paintings, with large Italian eyes and curly brown hair. His eyes were blue instead of brown and his hair was brown instead of black, but that worked. He sounded like family, too, like a Jew from the Bronx, like my dad. I didn't know about Italians from Jersey. He kept squeezing in next to me during the dances. Vinny, with a broken foot, sat in the corner and glowered. I found out later that he had broken his foot trying to sabotage a federal housing project that they were planning to build in the North Ward in Newark.

Afterwards, Anthony wanted to go for coffee, so we all went. Anthony, me, Vinny, Johnny, and Jane. I was flattered because Anthony, Vinny, and Johnny all walked me home. This was an adventure. Somehow Johnny left, and Anthony yelled at Vinny to go wait on the other side of the street, and he asked for my phone number. I told him Suzie wouldn't let me give it out.

So Anthony gave me his. I didn't have a chance. I entered the next chapter of my life like it was a recurring dream. He told me that he and his friends had a problem with drugs. How fun! I told him I thought I could fix that with Reevaluation Education. I had taken the class.

I called and asked about the group we were going to get together. After some hedging, he gave up on the idea of getting the group together and asked me out. I knew that the "group" was a ploy, but I didn't know if he knew that I knew.

Vinny showed up with Anthony on our first date. Suzie waited in the lobby with me until they came. She didn't want my dates to know which was her apartment. As we were leaving she asked me if I was sure I would be okay. "Of course!" I said.

After we left the lobby Anthony told Vinny to get lost. This was as good as "West Side Story!" We looked at children's books, and walked around The Village. I almost didn't notice when he took my hand, it was so comfortable. We sat in Washington Square Park, and neither of us wanted to say goodnight. Anthony said he missed the last train to New Jersey. I showed him the roof of Suzie's apartment house on Christopher Street. We stayed there until the sun came up.

He started coming to see me often. Sometimes he brought friends. Once it was ten of them. This was better than "Seven Brides for Seven Brothers"—Jane Powell only had seven. We often slept on the roof. He brought orange juice and wheat thins, later a bathmat for padding. When it rained we'd sleep in the elevator shaft. Once he interrupted a gay couple having sex on the next level. He hoisted himself up to see what the noise was about. I remember him in mid chin-up, apologizing graciously. I sang the entire score to "West Side Story" up there, straddling the wall of the roof. He would give up drugs with Reevaluation Education. I'd save all his friends, too.

A month later, we rented bikes and rode around the lake in Central Park with Bob Faella, one of Anthony's closest friends. Bob started pedaling after me, trying to convince me to stay in New York.

"Stay here," Bob said. "Don't go back to California."

"I can't afford it here!" I answered, pedaling faster.
"You can get a place with me," Anthony said. "We can split the rent." I tried to accelerate, but it was a really

beautiful day, the lake was sparkling, and Anthony was lagging behind, letting Bob do all the work.

"What about your responsibilities?" my mother asked on the phone, her voice reaching a pitch I hadn't heard before. "What responsibilities?" I asked, sincerely confused. "Your dog, your cat, the guesthouse, the car?"

I got a temp job and ate only Suzie's Fluffernutter and Christmas plum pudding (the two items she told me I could have all I wanted of) to save my money until we had enough to get an apartment in Jersey City. It was a fourth-floor walkup. My mom brought Gretel, my dog, and Marzipan, my cat, and because pets weren't allowed Anthony always carried Gretel downstairs and out the front door in his size 42 parka. The super could have been a character written by Dickens and only stayed in the basement. Marzy stayed in the bathroom, except for the time she caught a mouse, and Anthony locked them both in the closet until the scuffle was over. Marzy walked out alone, the victor. I was so hysterical she never hunted again.

The neighbors across the way gave us a mattress. I bought a mobile with colored paper butterflies that danced above it. Later we found a couch on the street. We could see the river from the kitchen window.

Anthony's friends came over, so I made tea and entertained them until he got home. They nodded in their chairs and made strange aerial gestures with their hands, like torpid birds. If Anthony did drugs I made his life hell until he stopped. I gradually turned up the bass on his speakers when he had his earphones on. I flew into rages, feeling betrayed. I went to stay at Suzie's.

We both got jobs at Gino's, a local burger place that was walking distance from the apartment. I had to wear a boxy red polyester dress, and Anthony had a matching shirt. A few weeks later the manager called the cops on

Anthony because they found a bottle of pills in his parka with six Gino's Giants. He had been hanging over the grill, in middle space, not frying burgers. His eyes were red and sunken, his lips slack. It was pretty busy, but he was in no condition to notice.

The manager discreetly told me that they had taken Anthony away. I rushed home, and our neighbor from across the hall went with me to the police precinct and posted the fifty-dollar bail. Anthony then told the judge off. "It was just a few lousy Librium!" he bellowed. I didn't like this movie. It was dark.

He used his parka when we went shopping for groceries, too. We'd buy the large items like a loaf of bread, a quart of milk, lettuce, and he'd pocket the smaller items like butter, cheese and spices, because the lining of the pocket was ripped, and the item would go from his pocket right into the lining of the coat.

I could never cook a whole meal without burning something, could never have everything ready at the same time. My housekeeping skills were surreal. Our first fight after we were married was about toilet paper. Anthony couldn't understand why there wasn't any. There always had been before. He went back to his parents' house for the day.

Suzie once said, "You can take the boy out of Newark, but you can't take Newark out of the boy." When I said I was going back to California, Anthony decided to come too. He never forgave me though.

We lived in eight homes, had two kids, five marriage counselors, and six pets, including Jennifer and Gefilte, the goldfish. They all eventually disappeared, except the kids.

We loved each other a lot, but ended up hating each other for what attracted us to each other in the first place. I loved having his strength on my side, but he too often became my enemy. He was better at war strategy. There wasn't the time or energy to reconnect. He became ill. I wanted to sing, dance, write and act. He always seemed angry at me. I didn't want a Chinese Restaurant, optical store, or real estate deal in Malibu. California and I took him away from his roots. I became afraid of his anger, closing myself off, and planning my escape. We didn't make it, but we did make amazing daughters. I must have known what I was doing after all.

14 INTRO TO ITALIAN

We took the tubes to New Jersey to meet Anthony's family. The tubes were fascinating, modern, and cool. We got off at the end of the line, Jersey City, and climbed down several flights of stairs to the city subway—a single little trolley car with crank windows that clattered and rattled along its tracks, in an abandoned canal through the beautiful green foliage. Newark was country! We passed through an exotic landscape of swamps, factories, and towns. L.A. only had scrubby olive chaparral—nothing like this! The trolley swung in a circle at the end of the line like an amusement park ride. I loved Newark!

I wanted to neck with Anthony on the subway. I couldn't stand it; he was too embarrassed. He was embarrassed on the way home, too. He never was embarrassed in New York, and I was a little stunned, but didn't want to acknowledge my hurt. The ecstasy of love was so much nicer, and I wanted to milk it. I was willing to block out the audience. I was trained to do that, and it made life so much juicier, although I'm sure that trait has contributed to my ability to make a spectacle of myself.

I didn't want to meet the family. Here we were at a three-family New Jersey house; three Castelluccio families, and I was going to die. Anthony pried me up the stairs. At the top I was met with almost frenzied approval; relatives came running from all corners of the horizon to see what Anthony had brought home with him. It was a girl. She looked like a nice girl. Was she Italian? No? Jewish? Well, that was okay, too.

I was given the largest bowl of macaroni I had ever seen and they actually wanted me to eat it all. I knew I could do it. They watched each mouthful and cheered me on. I loved the macaroni and the approval. Bring it all on! I'll eat anything you throw at me! They loved me. I was in. Anthony's mother was big and warm, his father was handsome and cool. His sister was a sweet-faced teenager who said "cute" all the time, and drew it out while her face went all over the place: "Cuuoooit!" His sister-in-law was dressed to kill, with a huge black wig, and long, shiny red talons and tons of makeup. She was very gentle and innocent. Anthony's brother was soft and shy and suburban, not at all taut and leonine and streetwise like my Anthony.

The three women waited on us. This was amazing. I had never seen anything like this before. Anthony changed his demeanor and stretched out like the Dauphin in *The Lark*, like someone who was used to being waited on. I had only seen this type of behavior in movie stars and psychiatrists and in very, very expensive restaurants, with three waiters hovering over the table. It was hard to chew. I kept smiling at them while my mouth was full of meatballs, to let them know that I was just like them, but the women only wanted the dinner to be technically perfect—the exact right temperature, timing texture, flavor. I had the full burden of having to know what my preferences were. I was impressed, but a little scared. No, Anthony says I'm a princess; he wouldn't expect me to be like these women: scuttling around and waiting on him. My God!

Anthony was my dream man. He treated me in a way that I had never been treated before. He really listened to me when I spoke and kissed me when I wasn't even expecting it. He always kissed back at me when I kissed him first. He was the most affectionate, responsive man I had ever met. He was interested in dance, too. He wanted to dance more. He was also interested in art. He wanted us to paint together. He even loved jazz—we were going to hear all the greatest. He loved to get out there. We were going to go—to move! We read children's books together. We sang together; we played together! And he was gorgeous. He had the head and body of a Michelangelo, and gray-blue eyes; and when he looked at me, he had the sweetest, gushiest, softest face I had ever seen, and I wanted to squeeze it and kiss it all the time.

We got a place together in Jersey City. I didn't eat for a week to save money for rent, just a little Irish Pudding and whipped marshmallows I stole from my roommate, and a little Greek food someone's mother from work made for us. Alone at last, closing our own cute door. No more sleeping on the roof or in the boiler room: we were now members of civilization. Cute little houses across the street. Jersey City wasn't the Asshole of Creation like my mother said, it had cute little houses across the street, and Anthony, and a view of some water in the distance. We borrowed a mattress from across the hall—our first furniture—and we closed the door.

If Anthony hadn't been addicted to drugs, the whole scene would have been close to idyllic. Picturesque. I was working, and Anthony was going to school. We were madly in love, except when he had red eyes. I didn't like his friends who "got high," an interesting expression for guys who sat with dull eyes, slumped over with sucked-in cheeks. They would come over when Anthony wasn't there, and I'd have them wait for him, making coffee and little sandwiches and listening to disjointed, rambling talk with weird gesticulations, while I tried to be the perfect hostess and not scream.

Getting high was a Newark custom for young guys who hadn't "settled down" yet. It was considered good/bad by the other guys, monstrous by the parents, and tragic by the girlfriends. The guys would band together and sneak out like mischievous little boys, covering up for each other. The girlfriends and mothers, and sometimes the fathers, would threaten, throw things and stay up all night waiting for the guys to come home. Most of the guys lived at home. Getting high was the BIG THING. It broke up relationships, lost jobs, flunked classes, gave police records, rotted teeth. It was sowing wild oats.

We had dinner at Anthony's parents' house every Sunday, but we didn't tell his parents we were living together, because Anthony wanted them to think I was a good girl. Freddy, his brother, and Etta, Freddy's wife, would say they were taking me back to New York every Sunday night, and Anthony would "go along for the ride." They'd then drop us both off in Jersey City. I hated the lie, so I started nagging. Anthony said he'd like to get engaged but wanted to wait until he could afford a ring. I told him I didn't care about that. I saw a ring for five dollars that I liked at Journal Square. It was silver and had a small flower on it. We bought it. I don't remember who laid out the five-dollar investment in our future, but now it was official. I could tell his mother while he hid in his old bedroom.

The following Sunday I stopped his mom in the kitchen, halfway between the sink and the refrigerator. I took a deep breath and blurted out, "Anthony and I are living together and I'm married to someone else, but we're separated, and Anthony and I are going to get married as soon as my divorce comes through." His mom stared at me a moment and then ran to the back window and shouted across the yard to her sisters, "Lulu! Marie! Anthony's engaged!"

My divorce from Tim came through and Anthony and I got married. Anthony's parents paid for the wedding. My mother wasn't going to come, but she gave in at the last minute. That was some wedding, at Beppy's, a large hall in Newark. We were half Jewish-Leftist intellectuals, half blue-collar Italians.

Can marriage work? We bought a new car with our wedding money, a Chevy Vega, orange with a sporty stripe on the side, and drove across the country with the dog and cat for our honeymoon. I wrote a song about Nebraska. Anthony studied for his National Teacher Exam. On the way home Anthony drove the Vega off the road, straight into a ditch. We tumbled, the car was totaled, and as I sat there, trying to decide if I was dying or not, Anthony was taking pictures of the wreck (the car). He told the highway patrol I was driving, because he had been driving without a license. I had a concussion. I threw up on the examining table. We flew back home and started our new life in Newark.

How quickly a face changes from soft to hard. A dandelion closes at night. Lots of flowers do. When Anthony's face closes I get a chemical reaction through my body and a taste of vinegar in my mouth. At first I'm panicky, thrown off-center, then when I get my balance back, it's from a new perspective, and I'm angry at the son of a bitch who deprived me of Anthony, my life, my sustenance.

I believe in love; although, for all practical purposes, the IQ in me can tell me any day of the week that the me that believes like that is a puff—a drooling imbecile who reads "Can This Marriage be Saved?" in women's magazines, the idiot that no one worthy of my love could love anyway.

"Can This Marriage be Saved?" almost always has happy endings: the husband stops screwing around, drinking and beating his wife. The wife learns to express herself in a more positive way. The husband learns to express his feelings, and goes into analysis to find out why he has to screw around and drink and beat his wife to feel like a whole person.

She, on the other hand, goes to college to become an elementary school teacher, and finds fulfillment and isn't as boring as she once was. She also stops being so goddamned nice, which is why he beat her in the first place. Anyway, they come to realize that life isn't a rose garden, acquire a more mature perspective, and live reasonably happily ever after.

I want to live happily ever after, too. I too have acquired a more mature perspective, but we won't tell anybody that I really don't give a shit about that; that was just for the purpose of being released from marriage counseling.

I'd been married for about six months. I'd get home from my job as a non-person.

"The house is a mess!" he'd say.

"It's not my job!"

"I didn't say it was your job; I said it's a mess!"

"Yes, but you implied it was my job by saying, 'It's a mess!' with anger, and not dismay!"

"Whose job is it anyway, if it's not yours? I suppose it's mine! She works one day, and Miss Lib says it's not her job. Big friggin' deal. Go back to California."

I feel so repressed. All my potential has been dormant for so long, it's in one big clot.

"Do you have a resume?"

"Name: Clot Castelluccio
Address: Clot Street, Newark.
Age: Aging fast.
Work experience: Non-person type of jobs: little things.
Education: The usual.
Height: You know, short.
Weight: Average: I eat too much shit."

My mother warned me. She got hysterical when I told her I was staying in Newark. I had never known her to be hysterical, but she was hysterical now. But, seriously, who listens to their mother? And when they're in love? My God. The mere thought of it goes against everything I believe in. Your mother? Are you crazy? What the hell does she know? Did Romeo and Juliet listen to their mothers? And they're immortal! Did Anthony and Cleopatra? Tony and Maria? Listen to your mother and you'll get to be 70 or 80, tops, with something to fall back on.

15 NEWARK

In Newark the people talk like they do in gangster movies. "Hey bay-bee (to men, not women). What's happenin'?" "What's the word!" (out the window), "Shoot any pool lately?" People have nicknames in Newark. Peanuts. Bastalluch. Juke. Skins. If someone doesn't have a nickname he's called by his last name. Women are called by their husband's or boyfriend's names, as in "Tommy's wife" instead of "Cathy."

Italian families (most families in North Newark are Italians) have a huge midday dinner on Sunday. The women do the cooking, serving, and cleaning up. The men watch television. The men in Anthony's family even watch television while we're eating. When I was given the place at the head of the table I was very touched—at first. It didn't take me long to figure out that it was because I was short and they wanted a view of the TV behind me. For four years the men in the family looked over my right shoulder for Sunday dinner. Every Sunday, pasta is eaten. When the games are not on, gory stories are told while we're eating the blood of the tomato.

NORTH NEWARK

North Newark is bound on the south by Bloomfield Avenue, where the straight Italian Stock starts to get mixed with Puerto Rican and Black. The property value goes down as the Italian population becomes thinner. The Italians resent having their neighborhood invaded. Along Bloomfield Avenue are the old stores that still sell barrels of olives; the bakeries where you can buy pizza dough, the butcher who knows how to cut bracciola, and how to pronounce it in Southern Italian. The old guard.

As you move south you get less and less Italian and then less and less Puerto Rican, until you are practically all black. That means you are in the Central Ward. Most women from North Newark haven't been to the Central Ward in years. There is some sort of ominous quality attributed to it. When we drive through it the car is locked. I am frightened in a nameless, boogey-man sort of way. Lots of windows are boarded up. People hang out on the streets, drinking . . . they talk with a different accent . . . there are masterless, aimless dogs . . . empty lots. There is one home that's decorated with hubcaps.

Back on Bloomfield, the Italian teenagers hang out and do what appears to be nothing. They are loud. The boys wear t-shirts and are well built. The girls look like whores and are mostly virgins. Good girls. They chew gum.

J.B., Vinnie's father, is a bail bondsman. He has a shop on Bloomfield Avenue. He will fix us up if we go to California. He knows people. Take care of us. Drives a new Cadillac. Bad looking.

Anthony's family lives in the northeast corner of North Newark, just where it meets Bloomfield and Belleville. Branch Brook Park runs along the border; a beautiful, graceful park with stone bridges, lakes, and cherry trees that are gorgeous and fluffy in the spring. They live on Beaumont Place, just where it meets Verona

Avenue. Beaumont Place is residential, with cute three-story houses with neat little lawns. Verona Avenue has a block of stores, just around the corner, before the tenements start.

The busiest store on Verona Avenue was the butcher shop. The butchers just moved. They had been there for thirty years. Everyone knew them. Now they're gone. The neighborhood is changing. One day Phil the deliveryman got held up. The story went that he had come in at six in the morning to open up, as he often did, when a young guy came in, pulled a gun on him, and Phil had a heart attack. No shot was fired, but Phil was in the hospital.

We were all aghast. All the talk was about Phil. Much later, a different story came out, apparently the real one. Phil had been robbed. When he made his deliveries he was so shaken up, and the neighbors so sympathetic, that at each house he had a "nip for his nerves." At the last house he was so crocked that he fell down the stairs and cracked six ribs. That's why he was in the hospital. There was no heart attack.

Next to the butchers is a store that was never successful. It had been a luncheonette, a pizzeria, and several times a candy store, but somehow it was jinxed. The rent was low, the business in the surrounding stores was good, but no one had ever found the formula for this poor little store.

The fence on the corner between Verona and Beaumont Place is gone now, too. The guys used to sit there. Now there's a cinderblock wall, about five feet tall. You can't sit on a five-foot cinderblock wall. The wall was covered with graffiti, but Nick, a neighbor, got sick of looking at it and painted it white. Nicky Caruso still hasn't painted his house. It is a pale and peeling pink. The lawn isn't mowed. The tenants are unkempt. They are foreigners. Nicky Caruso apparently had a vendetta against

Beaumont Place, where the houses were so trim, the lawns so mowed, the sidewalks so clean.

Next to Caruso was Maggie, who used to get mad at Anthony and call him "Bubble-eyes."

The Coultres live across the street. Nick is the one who painted the wall. "Big time." Cadillac. Always has a deal going. His son, Juke, is a cop. He has no hair. It fell out in clumps. He hates being a cop. Works part time at Danny's, the neighborhood hangout. Danny is a Jew. He has a little store where you can get everything from an ice cream sundae to a color TV set. Danny's nice. He said when we finally moved to California that we'd never stay there, that we'd be back in a year. Said there's no place like New Jersey. No place like New Jersey, he's telling me.

The Leaf Man

He stood in front of our new apartment house, tall and dignified. He was always formally dressed, always carried an umbrella. The garden apartment lawn was divided in two by a walkway. To the north of the walkway the lawn was covered with leaves and debris. To the south, the lawn was smooth and green and spotless. The Leaf Man looked over that half, poking at the earth with his umbrella. When he found leaves he would arrange them in a wreath around the fire hydrant on the south side of the lawn. When the wind blew, there he would be, industrious and frowning with self-importance . . . arranging and re-arranging the wreath, even though the wind would blow the leaves away as soon as he lay them down. He was always there, guarding the lawn. Once when giving directions, Anthony said, "Turn left on Heller Parkway, go three blocks to Forrest Hills Parkway, make a left and stop at the old man picking up leaves."

16 I'VE BEEN THINKING ABOUT UNCLE ANTHONY

I've been thinking about Uncle Anthony. He is so pure, so consistent in his tragedy that we can laugh at him. Uncle Anthony is in Overbrook, the state mental hospital in New Jersey. He is safe there from the constant comparison to 'functioning' people. When he is outside, their communication, eye contact and step-by-step behavior, is a source of awe to him.

He thinks about dying. He thinks about his son whom he is not allowed to see (His ex wants them to have nothing to do with him). He thinks about food. But most of all he thinks about the cigarettes, which are the supporting structure of his life. He believes in the cigarette ardently, and would sacrifice freedom, comfort, and the pursuit of happiness for it. He was kicked out of halfway houses for his careless smoking, of relatives' houses for burning furniture and carpeting, of the progressive wing of the hospital for his smoking in restricted areas.

His balls are in that package of Pall Malls soft pack, and he smokes with class, ardor and a thoroughness that I never saw before. He doesn't leave butts. His fingers are amber and burned. He has no teeth, but his gums are discolored. When he smokes he sucks his cheeks all the way in. His whole body becomes a syringe for the cigarette. The world is his ashtray. Sometimes Uncle Anthony was released from the hospital for a couple of days, and his brothers and sisters would take turns keeping him for the weekend. Once, when staying with Aunt Selma and Uncle Julio, he cornered Aunt Selma and asked if he could talk to her in private.

"Of course," Aunt Selma said.

"This is very difficult for me," said Uncle Anthony. "I don't know quite how to put it into words."

"Yes?"

"It's so terribly difficult for me to ask this of you. How can I say it . . .?"

"Say what, Uncle Anthony?"

"Selma . . . could I have a cigarette?"

17 GRANDMA ROSSI IS A SAINT

"Grandma Rossi is a saint," everyone in the family would say. "What's your grandmother like?" I asked Anthony when we had just met. "She's a saint," he said.

The first time I met Grandma Rossi, she was in the hospital, hardly able to see and had just had some frightening hallucinogenic experience with drugs the doctors had given her. She saw flowers all over the wall, but something about that scared her.

There she lay, this scrawny, little bird-woman who moved her hands like a young teenage girl who might sit on them at any moment, the way they flew all over the place. Her hands seemed animated with a life of their own. Her body was frail, her voice weak and chirping, but her hands were flamboyant, flirtatious, merry. Aunt Lulu had hands like that.

At the family gatherings at Grandma's house, when she got too weak to socialize she would sit in the bedroom, alone and folded, like a nylon stocking left on the bed. When someone talked to her, she would become inflated like a wind sock.

I would listen to her for hours at a time, not understanding much of what she said, but in love with the spirit in her. Sometimes Aunt Lulu or one of the sisters would come in to translate. Grandma Rossi would have been talking about her girlhood in San Lupo, about school plays, about ethnic music on the radio, about her late husband. I would just nod my head and say "uh-huh," when she paused for an answer. Sometimes I should have said "no," but her English was so broken that I was really floundering. When I said, "uh-huh" in the wrong place, she would shake her head and explain again—I wouldn't understand any better the second time, but eventually I got expert enough to bluff, to say "um," and then cover it quickly with a "no," or an "uh-huh" if I felt she was approving. Sometimes I would murmur all three tentatively, and see which one pleased her the most, then I would reinforce that one.

Grandma's daughters dressed her up and played with her. They put combs in her hair, sunglasses on her face, a trench coat, a wig maybe—she loved any kind of attention. When Anthony and I were engaged, she was schlepped to the middle of the floor, with Ant and I on either side for support, and she sang an Italian love song to the gathering.

One day when I was sitting on her bed, Grandma grabbed my breast and squeezed it, gasped and smiled, then after murmuring something in Italian she reached into her nightgown and pulled hers out. It was like half the foot of the nylon stocking: empty. She flapped it unabashedly.

When Grandma went to the hospital for the last time, the family was all in the lounge. She sent the nurse to call for us, and we came running to her death bed. She asked to be propped up, straightened herself out and burst into a round of "God Bless America." I miss Grandma Rossi.

18 I WAS OVER AT ETTA'S

I was over at Etta's when Freddy came home.

"You'd better call Mom. She passed some blood in her urine. Aunt Lulu and Aunt Marie are over there, but she's pretty upset."

Etta once had a bladder infection and had passed lots of blood. So I called. "See, Ma—and she's doing just fine! Here, talk to Etta."

"Ma, yeah, I had a bladder infection. I spent two nights in the hospital. It was nothing. It's not necessarily that serious to pass blood.

We'll be right over."

We drove to Ma's house. She was in the kitchen, pale and limp. Aunt Lulu, Uncle Vito, Aunt Marie, pregnant Michelle, Gene, Dad, Freddy, Etta, and I made a somber, consoling ring around her.

"Have you had dinner yet?" Ma asked.

"Yeah, we ate."

"What did you eat?"

"I don't know. Hamburgers and salad."

"Are you hungry?"

"No, we're not hungry."

She shuffled to the refrigerator. "I made these for dinner." She took out hot dogs dipped in corn meal and fried them. Delicious. "Weren't they delicious, Uncle Vito? Aunt Marie had some and so did Rosalyn. Weren't they delicious?" She walked around the kitchen with a tear-stained face, stooped over, displaying the hot dogs.

"Do you want some?"

"We're not hungry, Ma."

She cut them into little pieces. "Here, you've got to try them." We put them in our mouths. They were cold and tasteless, like impending doom.

Ma sat down and began to weep silently. "I just don't want to die before the baby is born," she sobbed.

We bowed our heads.

"I made some beets last night. They were delicious. Just a pinch of salt. I gave some to Aunt Lulu. Weren't they delicious Lulu? Weren't they, Vito?"

"Did you call the doctor?"

"Do you want some?"

"No, thanks. Did you call the doctor?"

"Yes, I have to go in at eight. Let me show you."

Ma went into the bathroom and came out with a paper cup filled with sickly pink fluid.

"What's that?"

"That's my urine."

"Oh, my god." We all bowed our heads.

Eight o'clock came around and Ma stood up to go. I kissed her goodbye and so did Etta, Aunt Marie, Aunt Lulu, Rosalyn, Michelle, Freddy, Uncle Vito, and Gene. She left with Dad, solemnly promising to call as soon as they got home.

The phone rang at 9:00.

I leapt for it. "Dad?

"Beets," he said.

19 MY FATHER'S OPERA

Dad was in no mood for cancer. He had a lot of things he wanted to do. When Dr. Belovski discussed the prognosis with Dad, Dad had one reaction: denial. Dad never mentioned the fact that he was terminal to any of us. He just went on with his work.

Dad had always been a re-writer. He had always been political, too. He was blacklisted for his political activity when he was an art teacher in the public schools. So by day he worked as a draftsman, but at night he wrote and re-wrote songs. He had a little lamp on his bookshelf-headboard so that he wouldn't disturb Mom. He would lie propped up against the books and update old songs to make them contemporary and political. He re-wrote "We Gather Together To Ask the Lord's Blessings" for Brotherhood Week. He re-wrote "You Are My Sunshine" to protest smog, and I was the only kid in the neighborhood who sang a union song to the melody of the ice cream truck.

Dad thought all his work was brilliant, flawless. No superlatives were too flamboyant, no praise sarcastic. In my adolescent naiveté and in my collegiate zeal I used to make suggestions from time to time. "Dad, I think 'cockeyed moon in a crazy sky' is a little corny, and nobody uses the word 'cuckoo' anymore." Dad's face would become dark, and a terrible, powerful expression would grow there. I was frightened. I waited for thunder. It was blasphemy again. I tried to laugh at him, but I didn't know for sure that he was wrong.

There was no escape, either. Sometimes Dad would follow me, singing his latest songs. If we were near the bathroom I would duck in and dawdle awhile, staring stubbornly at the pink tile, or thumbing through whatever ancient volume he had left next to the toilet. If I was in the kitchen I would look to my mother to save me. Sometimes she'd feed him, but that didn't always make him stop. He would often leap from the table and go get something to read or sing to us. I can still hear the abrasion of a badly tuned guitar and the hammering rhythm:

> "Old Beelzebub, old Beelzebub get off that apple tree!
> Don't you filibuster, buster, filibuster me!"

Sometimes his work was awful, and sometimes it was extraordinary, so that when it was awful, and I tried to laugh at him, I had a nagging feeling that maybe I wasn't hearing it intelligently enough, or with the right spirit, so I'd squirm through another session.

Dad started to lose weight. He knew it was just temporary. He started eating health foods, to take better care of himself. He didn't know what the world would do without him. Dad had been writing protest songs from the time of Hitler. While his brothers were fighting overseas, Dad defended the home front with his clipboard. When we fought segregation in the South, Dad's songs were sung on the marches. When there were lynchings or when the

KKK became active Dad would retaliate with a song. Now the Kennedys were dead, Reagan was running for office, and there was no strong opposition.

One day I went to visit. Dad was sitting in the backyard in front of a monument he had constructed from a concrete pillar set on a brick pedestal. Around the monument was a circle of white begonias. Around the white begonias was a circle of red begonias. Dad was sitting in an aluminum folding chair. He looked up when he saw me and his eyes went from philosophical to proud.

"What's up?"

"I've been meditating here," Dad said. "The white begonias represent the white corpuscles and the red begonias represent the red corpuscles. I'm going to see which overtakes which." I looked at the begonias, then at Dad, in his flimsy bathrobe. Was he really going to not exist, this force, this man who had enough anger and joy to fight for everybody, whether he knew them or not? Could I exist without him? There had never been space for me to think for myself. It took all the energy I had just to resist him.

"I'm working on an opera," Dad said, trying to get out of his chair. I tried to hold the chair steady as he rose to his feet and supported himself on the back. "I'm taking the mightiest music of all time, the best arias, mostly Italian. I'm going to strip Reagan naked, and expose the whole cabinet." He was now standing, looking at me like the angel must have looked at Joan of Arc. "I want you to produce it." I excused myself and went to the bathroom.

We heard that opera a lot that summer. Dad started rewriting his favorite arias. We gave him the feedback he had trained us to give. He was pleased with our progress. But towards the end of the summer he started hurting. When it got really bad we took him to the hospital. He wouldn't take any Percodan, because he wanted to be alert for his writing. His writing was good, but as pain started to control his body, the songs became even better—stronger, bolder than ever before. Eventually Dad's hand began to shake too much for his writing to be legible, so he had his visitors take dictation. They stopped bringing magazines and flowers. They came and sat down with a pencil. You could tell which was Dad's room when you walked down the clean linoleum halls of Kaiser Permanente. You could hear the opera all over the second floor.

One day in the early fall I went to the hospital. Dad had accepted Percodan and was in good spirits.

"You haven't said anything about producing the opera." I couldn't look at him. "Dad, I'm teaching full time; I have a family. I have a three-year-old. Dad, I can't. I just can't."

"Okay, I understand." Dad looked at me as if I had betrayed him. I understood too, but I didn't like it. Dad was dying with majesty and I was living with banality. I didn't have time to make monuments. I had to make the mortgage. Why couldn't I write all night like he did? Why did I need to sleep?

Soon Dad was sent home from the hospital with a lot of Percodan and three more arias. He wanted to be home. The hospital had no more ideas to try. We hired a nurse. She was Peggy, a born-again Christian with big bones and optimism on her face. Dad sent her out to buy a tape recorder. He called two old friends: Wally, a tall, thin, painfully shy man who played the organ at the Unitarian Church; and Jerry, a friendly, stocky many who promised he knew Italian opera. Dad also called me.

The recording session was scheduled for Dad's living room on a Tuesday afternoon in early October. It was a large room with a picture window looking out on the converted garage, now a guesthouse. The walls were covered with Dad's paintings and bookshelves filled with books that made me feel uncomfortable. Here were the worlds I couldn't enter. There were art books that I didn't appreciate enough; Renaissance paintings, shiny and somber; pages of narrative about modern works; and tiny black and white reproductions of color originals. There were old books of poetry that took a lot of effort to understand, and thick historical volumes. Volume No. III of Frederick the Great was missing. It was open next to the toilet. There were science books and political books. The Bhagavad-Gita was on the coffee table. The shelves were also crammed with international trinkets and crafts, assorted ceramics and sculptures done by friends, photographs, and awards. There was a shelf of books written by family members. I hated that shelf.

I was the first to arrive at the session. Dad was lying on the sofa in the corner, shrunken inside a royal blue velour robe that I bought him. I had hoped that if I spent enough money Dad would have to survive. The robe was holding up fine. The men arrived and we began. Jerry, the singer, didn't know many of the men's parts, so I had to sing some of them. Changing my voice, trying to be a tenor to the melody of "La Donna E Mobile" I was not what Dad had dreamt of:

> "Donate to Mobil Oil
> A well-spread global oil
> A pure and noble oil
> And so refined . . . "

Dad was getting frustrated with the way things were going and snapped that he would sing himself. We propped him up with cushions so he couldn't fall down, and we handed him the mike. He tried to sing, but was too weak. He said he couldn't because Wally, the piano player wasn't playing loud enough. Wally looked at me with hurt eyes and tried to be shorter. Dad thrust the mike back at me. At about 7:00 Wally said that he and Jerry hadn't had dinner yet and needed to leave. They would finish another day. I barked at them to sit down until they were finished. I had never talked like that to anyone before. I had to keep leaving the house and hyperventilate in the guesthouse where my mother and Peggy were hiding. I'd pace awhile and exchange looks with my mother. I knew I would calmly do what I needed to do despite the babbling in my head. When I could breathe again I went back into the house. To the Toreador Song:

"O torrid war
That's what I am for!"

Dad wanted my performance bigger, broader. It was supposed to be satire, but he wanted to make sure they got it. I was having trouble switching from the bellowing rogue to the ingénue, my pathetic thin voice trying to vibrate sweetly, the little notes not flowing as they were intended. Dad kept nodding out. I'd tiptoe up to him to see if he was breathing. Then he'd come to and snap orders at us. I'd jump back and try to breathe myself.

Finally we finished. The men quietly left. The house was still. Dad was out again. I went back and told Mom and Peggy that it was over. "Thank God," my mom said. "Why?" I asked? "Now he'll die." We went back into the living room. "Now let's take care of me," Dad said with his eyes closed. Mom and Peggy each put an arm around Dad and walked him to the bedroom. "Be sure to get it on the air before the election," Dad called to me from the dining room. "I will," I called back. They looked like a six-legged creature hobbling toward the bedroom: Peggy, big, sturdy and sure; Mom, small, faltering and stubborn; and in the middle, Dad, leaning towards Mom, slightly twisted, emaciated and unable to put his full weight on his legs.

The next day I was sitting in front of my class, teaching English, when a student walked into the room and left me with a memo saying in neat rounded letters, "Call home." I left my class to self-destruct and went to the office and called. Mom told me that Dad had gone into a coma. "Do you want me there?" I asked. "Yes," she said.

I got home somehow and Dad was lying on his side of the bed. He looked tiny. All of the power was gone. His eyes were not seeing and his mouth was slightly open. His face was smooth with wonder on it, like a new baby. I hated that. My only experience with death was in the movies. People lay on their backs, formal and dignified, under neat covers. I knew Dad would have preferred it like that. I sat on the bed and held his hand. It was cool and felt like loose twigs. "He's in a coma!" the nurse said enthusiastically. People started to arrive. My uncle wanted to call an ambulance. Dad breathed out heavily. "He's on his way!" the nurse said.

I had always believed that there was a precise time of death. But Dad's pulse fluttered for minutes after his last breath. I sat, holding his hand, studying the air above him for some sign of his spirit leaving his body. I waited a long time. I never did feel that separation, that special moment. Was it with his last breath, the last song, or the last flutter of his pulse? Or was it the moment, that one imperceptible moment when his rage died?

20 TROPHIES

I'm at East L.A. City College with Linda Mariscol, Eric Vo, and Jesse Rodriguez. These are my students and we're going to compete in the East L.A. College One Act Festival. It's my first time teaching drama and it's their first time performing. I can't believe how much I have invested in this. They love me. They trust me. They have never done anything like this before. The last time I was in a contest was ninth grade, and I broke out in hives so bad I was disfigured for hours. We're going up against "Stand and Deliver" Garfield, Wilson, and Roosevelt. I hate them. Elvia shows up to do "Hatful of Rain" in spike heels, skin-tight clothes, and hair in a huge, elaborate dyed bouffant. She looked like the other woman in a Mexican soap opera.

I wanted to say to her, "You're so stupid! How could you do this! You're supposed to play a simple '50s Gringatype American white girl goddamn housewife, Elvia. You're fucking history! They're going to crucify you! It's useless… I give up!"

I said, "Hi, Elvia. Is that what you're wearing? Did you bring anything else? No, it's okay."

And Jesse, who has the presence of Marlon Brando onstage. He's perfectly sincere, but doesn't understand what the hell he's saying:

"If I had known she was a *woman* like that I wouldn't of went with her."

"Jesse, it's a woman like *that*. It's not that she's a *woman*. It's that she's a woman like *that*. OK?"

Jesse is so gorgeous. He's been coming on to me for two years now. He uses his stuff to work me. I'm blank and professional as the sun.

"I stayed up to three working on my lines."

"Jesse, you're so great."

"I had a dream about you."

"You did."

"Yes. Do you want to hear about it?"

"I want you to run your lines."

And Linda's in her eighth month, doing "Fefu and Her Friends."

Linda's only sixteen, and has been living in the United States for about half that time. Her mother's Mexican, and her father's Puerto Rican. Her soft accent lies somewhere in between. She's drop-dead gorgeous, living with her boyfriend, graduating next month, and having a baby. The other teachers and her counselor have written her off. Linda's been telling me about her love life for a year now. Maybe she is doomed, but she sure doesn't know it. I want to be like her.

"Eric, let's run your lines."

"I'm a person, not a thing. I'm a decent, respectable, sensitive human being. I'm married now and have children, and I work for a living, just like you—you all know that. I have conviction."

"Eric, it's '*I do have convictions.*'"

"OK. 'I'm married now and have children, and I work for a living, just like you—you all know that. I have conviction.'"

"Eric, you've blown that very same line twenty times now. I swear if you blow it again I'm going to smack you with my purse."

"Yeah. Yeah. Yeah. Yeah."

"Run it again."

"I work for a living, just like you—you all know that. I have conviction."

Smack.

"I have conviction."

Smack.

"I have conviction."

Smack.

"*I do have convictions!*"

Jesus!

"Linda. You walk right up to the judges. Watch the expressions on their faces. You're talking to them. Feel what it's like to have them stare at you. Feel what you feel. Just be with it. I love you.

"Elvia . . . you're fine. All of you. I don't know what's going to happen. I just want you to know that I'd rather see you than any production I've ever seen. I don't know these judges. I don't know what they're going to think. Trophies aren't important. Horses get trophies. You're important. And what you've done is important."

My lower lip starts trembling and I choke back tears.

"OK, Linda, you're on."

Linda waddles up to the judges, glares at them, and lifts her head.

"I had been so deprived in my childhood that I believed the rich were all happy. During the summer you spent your vacations in Europe or the Orient. I went to work and I resented that. But then I realized that many lives are ruined by poverty and many lives are ruined by wealth. I was always able to manage. And I think I enjoyed myself as much when I went to Revere Beach on my day off as you did when you visited the Taj Mahal."

Roosevelt goes on; then Garfield does a message piece. I knew we were history because it was about this group of kids who were abused and they didn't wear makeup and I knew the judges would adore it. After that, the M.C. gets up and milks it . . .

"There are really no losers here today . . ." blah, blah, blah. "Each one of you is a winner . . ." blah, blah, blah.

"Best supporting actress . . . Lily Lopez. Garfield High."

Assholes. They don't know anything. She was abused and had no makeup and was just wearing jeans. Shit.

"Best actress . . . Betty Santiago, Garfield."

"No makeup, Elvia. T-shirt, abuse, drugs, gangs and juvy. How friggin' predictable. Stupid asshole judges don't know anything."

"Best supporting actor . . ."

"Shut up, you guys!"

"Eric Vo. Lincoln High School!"

"He got a trophy! Lincoln High School! Eric got a trophy! Eric! I'm so friggin' proud! Thank you thank you thank you. They are not totally stupid assholes. They have some insight. Fucking Garfield. Sh! Sh!"

"Best actor . . . Jesse Rodriguez. Lincoln High School!"

"They can see. Two trophies. Two very large trophies."

Then they gave me an enormous trophy that was displayed in the Administration building. It was for the school, but I kept it. It's in my classroom, with the ones for the next two years. It has graffiti scratched on the gold part.

21 GRANDPA

What's on my mind now is leavings. My uncle Joe, my mother's older brother, died this week. He was the last of his generation. My marriage to Anthony ended. I became a single parent. I moved from Los Feliz to the San Fernando Valley. I quit my teaching job. Relationships came and went, then I met someone whom I thought might last.

He left this week for a job in Northern California. I don't know where this leaves me. I know about endings, about getting on with my life; about taking care of me. I don't know about suspended animation, about waiting.

I'm about ten years old. Grandma and Grandpa live next door. They have always lived next door. Uncle Joe is here. Uncle Joe never liked me much, and he was a professional. I never liked him very much, either, although I knew I was supposed to, because he was a legend in the house. He's going to take them back to New York. They're old. Grandpa's got hardening of the arteries to the brain. (I'm ten and I know this.) Uncle Joe is an eminent psychiatrist. That is his full name. Even though we don't like each other we never acknowledge this because we don't have feelings in our family. Feelings are degrading. A Marxist family isn't concerned with the needs of the individual, but with the needs of society as a whole. The oppressed minorities have real needs. My needs typified those of the petty bourgeoisie. Besides, other people have it much worse.

The car is waiting in the driveway. I don't see Grandma. Grandpa is in the patio, saying goodbye. I snap and start crying and run and throw my arms around Grandpa's neck.

"Don't go!"

"I won't."

He goes, and I know that that will make him die. New York is taking them. They leave and become just stories, like the other relatives in New York. My mother told me that Grandma carried around one of my letters until it crumbled. Grandpa attacked Joe's wall with a hammer, saying that I was trapped inside and crying. I'm ashamed for all the trouble I'm causing. I think I'm supposed to write Grandma more, but she has a stroke before I get around to it.

My mom and I fly to New York. I tell my cousin Alice that I'm afraid I might laugh at the memorial. My Grandpa shuffles out to the podium set up in Joe's living room. He opens a folded paper and reads what he's written about

Grandma. I had never seen him look so sad; broken. Alice turns around in her chair to look at me.

"Are you laughing?"

The next summer we go to see Grandpa. He mutters all day in Biblical-sounding language. He's afraid if he stops talking he'll die. He thinks my aunt is collaborating with the Nazis. He calls her a "compromiser." Last year he was trying to break into cars on the street because he thought the Nazis were after him, and he didn't want them to know where his family lived. He can't go to the bathroom by himself. My mother and aunt help him, one daughter on each arm shuffling across the living room floor. Halfway across, he stops.

"You should notify the Olympics. I'm not ready. They should wait awhile."

#

I'm about five. My brother Alan is leaving home. He's eighteen. The car is waiting. He protected me from my brother Bob. Bob hates me and would like to kill me. I have chronic nightmares about running away from home to safety. I can go to Grandma and Grandpa's house for protection. I have no feelings as Alan's car pulls up the driveway, except that I want him to hurry and leave because I really have to pee.

My parents are leaving to go to a party. They're leaving Bob to babysit me. The car pulls up the driveway and Bob turns to me with a leer like from an old horror movie. This time I know I'm going to die.

#

So my boyfriend left Sunday. Ironically enough his name is Bob, too. I've done seminars, read books, and I know I should be happy for him. I'm not. I don't want time to work on me. I'm scared. I try to break up with him because I know how to start over after endings. That's my area of expertise; but being left behind in the same environment when someone moves on to fulfill his dreams . . . feels whiny and pathetic like Shirley Booth in a chenille robe and scuffies.

"You haven't called. It's been eight days. Come see me. I'll be rolling around on the floor, drooling and waiting for you. The cat's here. Say hello to the cat. Nesta, that's Bob, Nesta, she hears you, Bob!"

And then my conversation speeds up at hang-up time, and I make idiotic sounds to fill in the spaces to keep it going when I have nothing to say . . . "mmm . . . uh, uh, uh . . ."

Last weekend, Bob—my boyfriend—and I saw about a million dolphins. We were on a boat to Santa Cruz Island. They were leaping, flying all around us when I realized Bob had disappeared. I looked around the boat and found him at the bow, pointing to the dolphins and exclaiming something to a pretty blonde. I'm in the eye of a dolphin hurricane and I feel like there's a harpoon in my chest.

"There you are!" he shouts when he sees me. He runs to me and hugs me and kisses me on the head. The dolphins hurt now. "Go away blonde-thought; I'm having an epiphany!"

This morning on the way to work, I'm driving down PCH and I see a dolphin alone, very close to shore. I'm worried about it. It's not safe to be that close to people.

22 TRASHPLANTS ON THE 405

I was going to write the Great American Novel, but I
don't have an idea. Nothing. But that's why I bought this
voice-activated tape recorder, so I don't waste my time
when I'm commuting around L.A. I'm driving east on
Venice Boulevard on the way to my friend Alice's house.
I'm crossing Centinela. There's a man. No! She's not a
man! She's a woman with a black hat selling oranges.
Another woman's putting a mirror into the back of a
station wagon. There are two of her putting a mirror in the
back of a station wagon. There are a couple of puffy
clouds. The sky's pretty blue! And I'm driving towards the
smog.

I've heard it said that many people have breakthroughs
driving on the freeway, that it's like being on a river, or in a
shower, that thoughts start to flow. The only thoughts that
are flowing here are road signs.

*BODIES IN MOTION. YOU CAN REST
WHEN YOU'RE DEAD, FOLKS
WE DO WINGS
BREAK SHOPS
SPORTSBAR & RESTAURANT*

I need a manicure. I really do. There's an old woman with a walker, and another old woman that doesn't need a walker yet. There's a man with a ponytail in a jeep, with his hand hanging out the window holding a cigarette between his thumb and forefinger. Girls don't do that. Why do guys hold cigarettes differently? Why would someone hold something between his thumb and forefinger? Could that be a natural way, or is it for effect? He has an earring on his left ear and highlights in his hair. His hair is prettier than mine.

Driving east towards the freeway. And I've got to meet Alice in Altadena, and I don't know how to get there. The direct way is to go through Downtown L.A. I'm going to be stuck in gridlock. But I have the tape recorder so I won't be alone. I'll have an hour's worth of taped stuff. And then I get to play it back and see how I think and I won't ever be lonely because I'll have me talking to me:

Two signs next to each other, both of them saying the same thing:

LIFE IS A JOURNEY   LIFE IS A JOURNEY

Two guys in a silver BMW convertible, making a right turn in front of me. O.K, now where are my sunglasses? Here they are. What was it, lecithin? Lecithin helps memory. They're selling oranges there, and roses. Oranges and roses.

FESTIVAL OF THE CHARIOTS VENICE BEACH SUNDAY, AUGUST 3RD 11 A.M. TO 6 P.M.

I want to go.

Another guy's selling roses on the other corner. That's nice. I like seeing people selling flowers. I think there should be more flowers everywhere. I am taking a stand for more flowers everywhere! Yes. I will plant flowers in my yard.

405 FREEWAY

I'm entering the 405 Freeway. Don't know precisely how I'm going to go to Pasadena.

"Shut up!"

Somebody just honked at me. OK. I'm not going to let him pass me. That's for sure. If he's going to be that rude and impatient he's not passing me. It's gridlock on the 405 at 3:36. Friday, August 26.

ONE CAR PER GREEN

It's me! It's my turn! What are they called, those blue things; those bushes with the blue flowers next to the freeway, and then some with little yellow flowers and trash. It's like 'trashplants.' It's like plants that grow without water, thriving on trash and smog and exhaust fumes. My dad had those blue things planted in Highland Park and I remember thinking they were ugly. They're like the ones that the moths screw on; those funny little butterflies or moths, the little orange ones. There's some bottlebrush, scroungy-looking bottlebrush and really ratty looking furniture.

LEFT LANE BLOCKED AHEAD

OK. I already don't love talking to myself. It's weird talking out loud. I wonder if I'm being phony because I think maybe I'm going to write this up, or if it's like morning pages, though morning pages don't really feel phony. Now I'm behind a red BMW. This one's dirty.

SAN MATEO PETER PAN BMW

"Peter Pan BMW." Go figure.

TOXGARD ANTIFREEZE RECYCLING ON SITE

"ToxGard." Friendly name. I wonder if S-I-T-E- No, that's the correct spelling. Spelling Police. New Jersey plates. They're hanging by a thread, these New Jersey Plates. I'm between two red cars. Oh, there's an army truck! There are two army trucks! Three army trucks! Why do I get so excited when I see military? It's like a disaster. Here comes another army truck. One of those with the khaki covers. Camouflage. That's funny to see a camouflage truck on the 405. If it was an appropriately camouflaged truck on the 405, obviously it would be a red BMW convertible. Here comes another army truck. How many does that make? I wonder if something's happening. They're probably just going from one place to another. It's what we're all doing. Going from one place to another. Very slowly.

There's mattress stuffing all over the side of the freeway. Nobody's adopted this section of the freeway, that's for sure. There's a white Miata convertible. That's Ex-Boyfriend Bob's Car again. I've seen like ten a day. What does the license plate say? TKMATA. I hate vanity plates.

ECONORIDE DOOR-TO-DOOR SHUTTLE

Door-to-Door Shut-Up. God, it's obnoxious to keep talking. Now why did the freeway just start going fast? We're going east towards Los Angeles, but that's no reason for it to go fast. They've got a lot of trucks on the freeway. I'd like them to bar trucks on the freeway because I'm not a truck. Between seven and eight, only white cars on the freeway. Between nine and ten, only blue cars. That would be the ticket. I want to impinge on your civil rights in silly ways. You can get a ticket if you're in the wrong colored car. That would be so interesting. To be on a freeway you would have to be a green car. Between seven and eight, green only. I'm not worried about the implications. I'll just put it out there. Have them do it for a week. We did something like that during the riots.

NATIONAL BLVD.
OVERLAND AVE.
CALL BOX
EXIT
ROBERTSON
LA CIENEGA
FAIRFAX

Well, it's been over an hour, and the only profound thoughts I've had so far are signs.

No wonder I'm bored. I have nothing interesting to think.

23 MARIA

After my affair with Jorge ended, my brain, my heart, and my actions were owned by a foreign agent. I don't know who made me wait in James's classroom for a glimpse of Jorge. I don't know who got me past the lawn where he sat every day. I was feverish, and didn't know how to access the Me that had always worked, and always cooperated with myself.

I asked Annette how to get through the day. She said, in that Annette way of hers, "Try smoking and drinking!" I tried, but it took too much concentration. I spent a lot of time watching "Lady Blue" on TV or "Family." I could also watch MTV. It was a new pain that I felt. It didn't seem to have an end, and I couldn't break free of it.

I remember my daughters bringing me runny Mother's Day eggs on a tray. I was sitting on the toilet, weeping. Rosie was about five, and Hannah was nine or ten; I put some of the egg in my mouth and tried to wash it down with tepid, loving tea.

A neighbor suggested a shrink to me, and I went. Annette suggested another shrink, and I went to him too—one on Tuesdays, the other on Thursdays. What the fuck, right?

I have a clear recollection of sitting in the middle of the classroom where I taught English as a Second Language in Lincoln Heights. The girls were trying to do something with my hair, and were putting makeup on me. We had taken a break from my lesson for the day. I had put them into groups to discuss questions like, "What is the meaning of life?" and "What's important?" Every answer they came up with got a "Why?" response from me. People would walk into the classroom; I think I had depressed pretty much everybody by then, and the kids would be sitting in groups, their heads in their hands, staring into middle space.

That's about when I started seeing Jorge hang out with Maria. Maria was a teacher's assistant as well (like Jorge) and she seemed casual with him. You could see the open, free, happy, uncomplicated friendship blossoming there. I felt like a sewer rat, or a mangy Mexican dog, haunted and sneaky.

Maria was, of course, just a kid. Jorge said she wasn't interested in him—she wanted a man with money. Was she shallow and materialistic? Could I do that? One day Maria was standing in front of me in the line at the cafeteria. She was wearing a denim mini skirt, denim jacket, and red high heels. I felt like an ugly, fat girl scout turned into a matronly middle-aged school teacher wearing hand-me-downs; haggard, sexless, left-over and drained. The only clear emotion I had was envy.

I had a dream about this Maria torturing me in some offhand way. Shrink #2 told me I needed to buy red high heels. I took Carol, my colleague, who was also seeing Shrink #2 (I turned eight of my friends onto him), with me to shop for shoes. I bought red high heels, and she bought red suede boots. I went home and immediately came down with the flu as punishment.

One day after school I saw Maria getting into a Nissan Pulsar, taking off the t-top, and shaking out her long straight hair (that went way past her butt). My hair was kinky and rude, and nothing happened when I shook it. She took off, hair flying, and squealed around the corner. I got into my Honda Civic station wagon, and went to pick up my kids from school.

I sold my station wagon and bought a Pulsar, sobbing as they wheeled away my car, my ten-year-old daughter watching me patiently. It had been a good car; it wasn't its fault.

I quit Shrink #1 and started going to church and taking aerobic dance classes at the Jewish Center. My teacher was in the middle of a divorce. Her husband was a judge. I asked her if he had been at all judgmental. God, how we danced. I started going to the gym, and dressing slutty and going out dancing with other desperate single women. I discharged my Shrink #2, who after two years told me I should be a stand-up comic. I said, "Fuck you." He said to bring him five minutes of material. He had connections. I brought him five minutes about someone who was on the edge, and poured her heart and soul out for two years, and her shrink told her she should be a stand-up comic. He said it was brilliant. I said, "Good bye."

Freshly inspired by church, I told my class to live their dream, that the time was now, and the place here; not to put it off. One kid asked, "What happened to you?" I said,

"You're right," so I quit, sold my house, and moved to the Valley, where I could go to church all the time, and not have to see Jorge or Maria.

I took aerobic dance twice a week, got hired by an improv acting company, taught in the community colleges part time, and drove the Pulsar with the top down, blasting Cumbias from the tape player. When my daughter totaled the Pulsar I bought another convertible, and then another, and wore the red high heels until a podiatrist told me I had hammer toes and needed to stop.

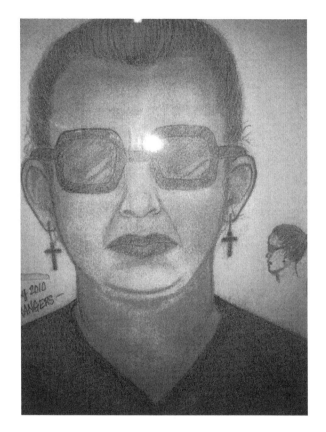

24 AMERICA

There were a lot of gangs at Lincoln High, but I was oblivious to them in my little bungalow, trying to drag responses out of a not-so-enthusiastic third period.

There was this one kid in English 10A who was a lot taller than the rest. When I first saw him I went numb for a second. He was about six-two and looked mean. He had the East L.A. gang walk, and eyes that didn't quite focus together. Inmate eyes. He turned out to be my most cooperative student.

I don't remember his name, and I'm edgy about using a pseudonym, because I might be right. I'll call him Jose. I hope that wasn't his name. There was another kid in my class who was a pain in the ass, Robert. That was his real name. Robert had just reached puberty, was small, twitchy, squeaky, and irritating as hell. When my friend Kathy taught at Lincoln I used to trade the "Roberts" for loud gum-snapping cholas with too much makeup. She couldn't stand those girls, but they didn't bother me.

Now I'm in front of the room being inspirational like Robin Williams in "Dead Poets Society," and Robert is being a pain in the ass, squirming and annoying the people around him. I didn't want to deal with Robert and break my concentration. I was very inspired and moved by what I was saying.

"You see, each one of you is special. Each one of you is unique. What you have to say sounds ordinary to you, but, trust me, if you're coming from a place of honesty, it's not. It just *sounds* ordinary to you because you're used to the way you sound. You're used to thinking these thoughts. We're not used to your thoughts, so if they're your true thoughts . . .

All of a sudden Jose leaps from his seat, flies across the room and grabs Robert by the throat, screaming, "I'm going to kill that motherfucker!" The next thing I know I'm standing between them holding them apart and there are flailing arms and fists everywhere. I pull Jose outside (I still don't know how all this is possible), and say, "You stay there!" I run back into the classroom, tell my assistant to take over, and without knowing why, grab a legal pad, pen and a volume of poetry.

Ginsburg. "America." He says "fuck." He's very angry. Yes. What the hell am I doing? Oh my god oh my god. This is insane.

I rush out to the patio and Jose is pacing, ready to explode.

"Sit down, Jose."

"I'm going to kill that little asshole!"

"I feel like killing him, too. I know. Now sit down, Jose!" I said. "You can't just kill people who get on your nerves. You get put away for that. But you can write about it. You can kill the paper with words, and if the words are strong enough, sometimes people get published and become famous, or sometimes they can create huge changes, just with words."

I pull out <u>Howl,</u> open it to page 31.

"America.

America, I've given you all and now I'm nothing.
America, two dollars and twenty-seven cents January 17, 1956.
I can't stand my own mind.
America when will we end the human war?
Go fuck yourself with your atom bomb
I   don't   feel   good.   .   .   "

"It says that?"

"Yes!"

"Let me see." Jose reached for the book and looked at the page I was reading from.

"Now you write, Jose. The angrier you are, the better. Just put it down on paper, and if it's any good, we'll look into getting it published."

I gave him the legal pad and the Bic and said, "Write. I have to go back in the classroom. I'll check on you when the bell rings."

When the period was over and the bell rang I went outside to check on Jose.

"Can I keep writing?" he asked.

"Yes," I said, feeling the goofy fear of breaking the school rules, tapping into Jose's rage for inspiration. At the end of the second hour he handed me the pad, heavy with anger and chewed by his pen. I told him I'd lock it up for safekeeping, and I'd take a look at it, then tell him what I thought. At lunch I opened the filing cabinet and took it out.

"Then we're going to really fuck him up, and me and Bobby are going to . . ."

I dropped it back into the file cabinet.

Jose came the next day and asked me, hopefully, what I thought. Once again I felt chicken shit. I had built him up, and now I was letting him down. Another copout for the establishment.

"Jose. This is evidence. If I read this I'm knowing some stuff I'm not supposed to know. I think you should keep this, but don't let anyone read it. I shouldn't know these things."

Jose took the tablet. I never had trouble with him again. Later I heard from a student that Jose was marked by another gang.

"What does that mean?" I asked.

"They're looking for him to kill him."

"Can we do anything?" I asked.

"No."

The next time I saw Jose I asked him about what I heard. He smiled and shrugged.

"Can I do anything, Jose?"

"No," he said.

"Well, I can talk to the dean." Jose smiled at me.

Later that day I found the dean, who was an actor in his spare time. "Ramon, I hear Jose is marked by another gang."

"That's what happens when you get involved with gangs."

"Isn't there anything we can do? Can't we find a place for him to go where he'll be safe? Can't we do anything?"

"No. And you're looking for trouble yourself if you get involved."

Not long after that Jose was thrown out of school for fighting. I don't know what became of him.

25 THERESA

Theresa was my mom's best friend. I called her my godmother, although both of us were part of an atheist community. I spent weeks at Theresa's house when I was small, without feeling homesick. Her husband, Sam, was a sculptor, and my father was a painter, and we both had homes with a lot of creativity and dysfunction.

Theresa's personality was sunny, wise, and sympathetic. I always felt accepted and understood by her. When I was small, her love felt a bit smothering. She would squeeze me and kiss me a lot. I wasn't used to this, and felt squirmy and uncomfortable. She would also want to take a bite out of my weekly hamburger. She was the receptionist at the dance school that I attended. My dad bartered dance lessons for art. I don't know if he actually did any art for Dance Center, but I had dance lessons for years.

This wasn't cute tap dancing like Shirley Simpson from Buchanan Street School did. It was modern dance, and there was nothing flirty about it. Just as my mother didn't like me to use coloring books, Dance Center didn't have us use cute scolding moves, throwing one hip to the side and shaking a finger at the audience. Dance Center wasn't like the musicals that I loved; we didn't use batons or twirly skirts. We had to be creative. There was seldom any coloring between the lines here, and I longed for lines to color between.

My parents would drive me there early Saturday mornings. We often were late. The train on Riverside

Drive had a tendency to stop us with minutes to go until class began. My dad would curse and hit the steering wheel, and my mother would try to calm him.

I wasn't grateful. I never felt like the lessons were for me. It was just another one of my duties, like drying the dishes with my brother, while my dad sang the same songs, every day, puffed up like a Mastiff.

"Young Molly who lives at the foot of the hill

Whose name every virgin with envy doth fill

Her beauty is blessed with so ample a share
Men called her the lass with the delicate air."

The harmony was the same too, meal after meal, year after year, with my brother Bob flicking a wet dishtowel at my butt. When I got stomach cramps and had to run to the bathroom, which often happened after dinner, my dad was sure that I was feigning it to shirk my responsibilities. I didn't feign things. I was serious about being a comrade, working together for the common good. I just wished the common good wasn't so annoying.

Dance Center was another opportunity to be part of the community.

Mom would leave me with Theresa, and after class I would go down the street to buy a hamburger. This was a special treat for me, and the hamburger was spongy, and covered with wonderful mayonnaise. Nothing like my mother's stews, soups, or Wheatina.

Theresa would always ask for a bite, and this, for me, spoiled it. She would leave a red lipstick print on a damp semi-circle, where the perfect white sponge was permanently crushed and bruised. I didn't want to hurt her feelings, and ate carefully around the damage.

Later, when I became a teenager, my mother signed a form making Theresa my legal guardian so I could go to Marshall High School. Our family was moving to Silverlake from Highland Park, but this wasn't going to be for several months, and I was supposed to live at Theresa's until the move was final.

I don't recall ever being signed back to my parents, although I did move back in with them after escrow closed. If I felt tolerated at home, I felt accepted at Theresa's. She called me her second daughter, but I knew that Diana, her daughter, held the number one spot. Theresa would mortgage her house to give Diana money. I knew I would be fed and given a sofa to sleep on, but I would never expect money from Theresa. I didn't expect it from my parents either.

A special bond developed between Theresa and me around frustration with my mother. Theresa understood, more than anyone, how my mother could be difficult, critical, unforgiving. This helped keep me sane. When the home is the universe it's hard to grasp what's fair, unless someone on the outside can give you perspective. Here Theresa was mortgaging her house to help her daughter. When I wanted to apply to The American Academy of Dramatic Arts, my mother wouldn't lend me fifty bucks.

Theresa had a degree in Art from New York University, but she never did anything with it except doodle. Her house was full of her kids' art and her husband's sculptures, though. The living room wall was covered with a huge Jackson Pollack-ish piece done by Butchy, whose name became Simon when he started high school. There was Sam, her husband's metal sculpture of a rooster, and a marble sculpture of John Brown cradling an infant. Diana had painted a corkboard with a wild paisley and flower design for Theresa's jewelry, which was pinned on it. She had papier-mâché figures in bold acrylic designs poised on tables and shelves around the room.

The art in my house was somber and gloomy. It was mostly in earth tones. The portraits looked haunted and morose. After posing for a couple of them I knew why. It was torture to stay still for hours on end and be scrutinized. The portraits of me had angry, intense eyes.

All Theresa had of herself in the living room was the magnificent and fanciful doodles by the telephone. Those, and the cat. The cat was an expressionless gray tabby named Kitty that she adored. I never understood why.

The kitchen was Theresa's room. We would get into our bathrobes and eat an entire watermelon there. She had enchiladas, brown rice with chicken and vegetables, sweet potatoes with sour cream, fruit from the trees in the backyard, tea with honey, and huge salads. She always fed me, and seemed to love to. I can't even muster up that kind of generosity with my own children.

When I divorced Anthony and started dating I realized that what I had to give in return was my drama, my adventures that I spun for Theresa, trying to make my pain colorful and amusing for her. At one point it hurt too much, and I couldn't talk anymore about a painful breakup. Theresa was on the phone, asking me question after question, and I said, "I don't think I can be your friend right now, Theresa."

She never forgave me. When she was sick and dying I couldn't rekindle our relationship. I had broken it. I tried to, but the conversation on the phone didn't flow anymore. She was polite and curt.

I had a dream one night of Theresa walking over a hill. It was dusk, and I called to her but she didn't turn around, then she disappeared.

I can't take it back. I can't be a friend to Theresa now, but my life has been about listening to teenagers, buying them crap from the school cafeteria, sympathizing when their parents are being jerks, and eating watermelon in my bathrobe.

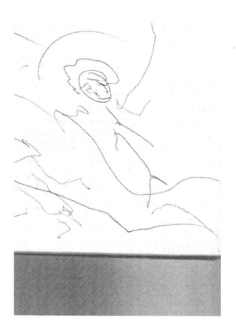

26 HAPPY NEW YEAR AGAIN

Although I declared myself brand new, I ate too much since midnight, drank too much, kissed the wrong man, fought with Rosie, and dog-eared this pretty journal that Hannah gave me. I'll just have to be new again, and again and again.

I think my house must be out of feng shui. I can't seem to spend any time in the living room. It's not comfortable.

We're landing in about twenty minutes. I can't wait. I love to land. I love to take off. I love to be there. I'm starting to be happy. I'm in love with the sunset, with Hannah, with Jorge Arturito, my new friend who's three. The stewardess is getting me café. I'm not in L.A. I'm in the air. Above Mexico. We're bouncing like we're about to start descending.

We found a bungalow with a view of the lagoon, and five beds. It's late, and everybody's asleep but me. It seems

I left my book on the plane. My feet hurt and I itch. I hear crickets and the fan. No cars. The view is gorgeous. I'm going to smoke. I love being here with the girls, and I'm not longing for anyone. The light from the window is making lines on the paper. Psychedelic college-ruled. I could meditate.

Crickets and a fan.

"La Bamba" from the club next door.

Balmy New Year's night.

I am new. I am new. I am new. I am a desirable woman who will have a committed relationship by January 20.

I'm happy here. The kids are happy here. I'm smoking my last Delicado. I had a dream about a puppet whose head fell off. Metamorphosis. New underpants. Feel like napping. Gentle place. It's the part of me that's gentle, innocent, and kind. The people. The girls. Are they melting yet? They put a lot of time into looking good. I did too. Looking out at the lagoon. The beauty is starting to set in.

Palms.
Lanchas.
Multi-colored umbrellas,
Hovering sun.

Is that the West? It looks mostly South to me.

Palapas on the island.

I want to eat quesadillas, ride the banana boat. Had two piña coladas. They were the best I've ever had.

You are the thoughts of the universe.

I have *la turista*. It's amazing. Better than fen-fen. Want to sleep. Can't, damn noisy room. Yelling Mexican *familia*.

"Onde vas?" Someone kicking his/her way across the pool. The girls and how they look. Did I forget or was I ever like that? Karine and her boys. Hannah and her magnet.

"Subete! No mas una!"

Me and my wanting to be alone. I don't know if I'll ever eat again. They keep me up at night, then wake me in the morning. They go to worship the sun. Me? I worship sleep. Loud family. *The Loud-osos.* Screaming now. Loud paradise without towels. And the toilet doesn't work. *Paradise Loud.* Two of them are screaming now, and the mother. Unbelievable.

"Memo!"

Shut up!

View of bamboo. Screaming and splashing. I never shit that much in my life. A horse couldn't have done better. Shut up! Casa Blanca next door. That's what takes care of the noise at night, the music from Casa Blanca. There are no single Mexican men my age. Maybe they're all in L.A. There goes my stomach again. What was it that I ate that the girls didn't? Lasagna? The lasagna of death.

I'm going to be in a committed relationship by January 20th.

That's two weeks. I've blown off so many men. Puerto Vallarta had towels. Plenty of them. Can they stay at the pool all day?

Lagoon cranes.
Birds.
People speaking enthusiastically in English.

A man in the pool.
Clattering plates.
Romantic Mexican music in the distance.
A lancha.
The new resort.
A couple talking next to me in English.

Don't make me listen to them. They're not my thoughts. They're theirs.

My legs are so hairy. They're discussing Hawaii versus Mexico. A shiny black bird. God, people annoy me. They're here in "Barra de Navidad" talking about cross-country skiing, hunting season, taxes, and all their money going to social services. No one panhandling here, just a pelican trying to get the fish the chef was filleting. It's about noon, and the girls are still asleep. I don't like Puerto Vallarta anymore.

I love the pelican.

I prefer to hear Spanish. It's softer, and more compatible with the gentle tropical . . . snorkeling in the swimming pool. Hannah wants to keep the name Castelluccio for her children.

Wolf.
Birds.
White geranium.
House plants blooming.
Two spider monkeys.
A parrot.
Two boats.
Palapas.
Red hibiscus.
Sand.
Bricks.
Painted concrete.
Palms with white trunks.
Cabanas at the resort.

Elephant ears.

(Only Spanish.) That comic book *fue divertido. Estudio el espanol para pasar el tiempo.* (Not lonely.)

I'm going to be in a committed relationship by January 20th.

Karine: That guy last night had pretty teeth.

Rosie: I wouldn't call them pretty; I'd call them politically correct.

I want to talk to my mother. I have no mother. I want a mother.

He has the sea in his eyes. I want the sea in my eyes, too.

I needed to create a vacuum. Now I want to close the vacuum. Confront my own emptiness. Empty is okay. It will pass. Tired will pass. Horny will pass. Life will pass. I love creatures. I had one once, but she ran away.

I'm eating to fill the void. The word void sounds like what it is. Om. Rain. I am Al the Holic. I'm just tired of tired. I'm not really scared of the void, just reluctant. I have nothing to wear. Despair of *ropa.* Clothes *schmertz.* I am my clothes.

I'm finding it particularly disagreeable to confront my emptiness. No one amuses me.

I'm going to dye my roots. Being dressed would mean I'm not crazy. When I was two I asked a waitress in a diner for "Non-carbonated dioxide." Everyone laughed. I was trying to say it right. I always just wanted to say it right.

#

I am so attached to my house now. It's not too messy. I'm happy here alone with Olive, the cat. I really do love being with me the best. I like myself. I stand on solid ground there. I am as I should be. I am as I am.

CORDOVA

My Head

My head feels like it doesn't belong to me.

There is something in me that's annoyed by my thoughts.

I'm tired of my complaining

Tongue-in-cheek doesn't make it okay today.

I have everything I want, so my body flicks its age.

My Lab is shaking a branch at the cat.

Try, Champa. Shake it harder.

You haven't learned cat talk.

You keep wanting her to be a dog and play like a dog.

Be still and know that I am Cat.

The paper is gorgeous.

The pen drags across it like an anchor on barnacles.

Mary Stewart put her head on the block. It took three blows to separate her head from her body.

I prefer yoga.

27 AMADO

Amado is one of the most irritating people I've ever known. He makes strange noises when he's eating. He takes his bridges out and sucks on them when we're in the car. He can carry on entire conversations without hearing a word I've said.

Me: Amado, I'd really like to sell the house this time. We could buy a little house in Austin for the winters and a little house in Portland for the summers.

Amado: A house in Austin and Portland. Okay.

Me: You could get maybe a part-time job teaching at a community college in Austin. We could spend more time together. You could study geology.

Amado: Um hum.

Me: You're not listening to me.

Amado: Yes I am; you said, "We could spend more time together."

Me: What else did I say?

Amado: Something about a house in Austin and one in New York.

Me: I didn't say anything about New York. I said Portland!
Amado: What about my job?

Amado will answer appropriately, considerately, even, and has become deft at his answers by now, but I often find out that he's been thinking about plate tectonics or glacier movements the whole time and hasn't heard a word I've said.

Amado is ten years younger than me. He's got a PhD in electrical engineering, which isn't really electrical engineering, because he doesn't know anything about circuits, just applied physics. He was the top student in Mexico, his mother says, the year he graduated from high school. He says that that wasn't true; he was only one of the top six.

Amado majored in physics in college in Mexico, getting a 4.0 average. No one has done that at The Universidad Metropolitana since. He got a degree in Paris that he thought was the equivalent to an MS, but we don't know what it was, and his PhD from Stanford. The first year was paid for by the Mexican government and Amado worked for the rest. Amado's father paid Mexico back, but by the time he did, the peso was so devaluated that his PhD came to something like ten thousand dollars.

When I met Amado, I didn't want my family to meet him because he was so conservative. He worked in aerospace and had aviator glasses. They liked him better than me. He seems like a nerd, a mama's boy, but I've seen him climb scaffolding and trek six miles in the desert without hesitation. I've seen him scale a cliff on the back of a pretty powerful horse, reigns in one hand, riding tall, and taking charge. I was on a nasty old thing that bit other horses and refused to move.

When Amado's working, he's cranky. He gives himself to it, and I get the ashes that remain at the end of his day. His face is nasty. He makes little balls out of napkins and flicks them around the house. He looks at me like I'm a thing, a nuisance. Once I filmed him like that, then sprayed him with medical marijuana, and presented him with the before and after videos. He recognized his grandfather, a math teacher from The Basque country in Spain in the first video. He decided to have a few glasses of wine when he started feeling better. I videotaped the third phase, when he became a Don Juan. I kept all three on my computer for ammunition until it was stolen a couple of years ago.

When Amado's not working, and/or when he focuses on me, I become all mumsy and complacent. He is my ideal man. He's brilliant, handsome, creative, and dances wonderfully, like Fred Astaire without taps, but with Mexican swivel-hips.

They say that there are seasons in a relationship, that particularly in Southern California we don't get this. When the autumn is coming in a relationship and the leaves begin to fall, we think it's over. The romance is dead. We don't get that if we keep vigil, new leaves will sprout again in spring. Amado will write me a poem, make me laugh, say something stunningly heartfelt (or so it seems).

Amado supports me. I retired early, and he pays the mortgage. He pays whenever we go out for dinner. He tries to pay when it's a group of people going out because he knows this makes me proud and happy. When he meets people, he's truly interested in them, what they do, who they are. He can't fake that stuff. He asks them questions. I talk about the food, the view, the waiter.

I don't know why I had the kind of standards that kept me alone for all those years. He had to be musical. He had to have a great sense of humor. He had to be blah blah blah. I think Hollywood and Cinderella did a tap dance on our expectations. I wanted to be swept away. Amado doesn't sweep me away, but he sweeps the patio and does the dishes. He cares about my happiness. He goes the extra mile.

Sometimes, when the light's right, Prince Charming Brando—warm, intuitive, sexy, and manly—is there before me with muscles, hairy chest and all the right moves.

Our marriage has all the seasons: winters of dislike, sexless and annoyed; spring of hope and rebirth, tentative and shy; summer of ease, warmth, fulfillment and rest; and fall, of seeing all the progress seem to slip through our fingers, followed by disappointment and sometimes despair. This season feels solid and warm, appropriate for August.

28 SPANISH FOR BEGINNERS

It's hard enough to survive in my native tongue, in my community with my countrymen, on my native soil. I spend an inordinate time feeling foolish, but to be around educated Mexicans for family holidays, visits and events I often feel like an imbecile. I know this is a universal condition for people who step out of their environment, but the look of patience and confusion that others get on their faces in Mexico when I'm trying to explain the simplest thing, like my political views, is unbearable.

Since I don't have the guts to be an expatriate, I married one. I've felt superior culturally, linguistically and socially. Amado said "an U-turn" for about ten years, even though I berated him a lot. He still says, "lay down" when he should say "lie down" even though I bust him on it all the time.

Amado makes educated mistakes—smart mistakes. I know what they sound like in English, but don't know what mine sound like in Spanish, and my judgment of his mistakes in English makes me insecure about mine. Amado will say something like, "Yesterday night" instead of "last night." That one pisses me off. I've told him that it sounded childish. Amado doesn't distinguish a blackberry from a blueberry, and his contempt for whatever difference there might be really offends me. He also doesn't distinguish between Asian people, which has made me get shrill on more than one occasion. I asked him how he would feel if I didn't understand the difference between the people from Guatemala, for instance, and the people of Mexico. He replied that there weren't, although I suspect he said that just to win.

I guess the distinctions in culture between physics and electrical engineering are as nebulous to me as the distinctions between Vietnamese and Cambodians are to him. People always tell me how brilliant he is and I want to yell at them, "He doesn't know the difference between a boysenberry and a raspberry!" He tells me they don't have these berries in Mexico, but I suspect that's just a copout.

Amado is much more generous about my inadequacies in science. Sometimes, in the bathtub, when Amado's trying to get to sleep I get inspired, and go running to make sure he doesn't fall asleep until I tell him my brainstorm about how he can win the Nobel Prize. It generally involves him doing the legwork, and often occurs after I've smoked pot.

Mucous, Amado! I bet that's why cancerous cells can enter healthy cells! I bet mucous has some kind of conductor which allows the semi-permeable membrane to be semi-permeated! Remember, they said that cancer cells thrive in mucous!

Amado will tell me how smart I am, and that it was a valid hypothesis and consider it gravely, then tell me he really needs to get to sleep because he has an eight o'clock meeting the next day.

I got back to the tub to finish brushing my teeth, dejected because inspired moments like that, say with Paul Muni and *The Life of Louis Pasteur,* never end like that.

He and his meetings. I didn't tell him to work for Rand Corporation. I have a one o'clock Pilates appointment and you don't see me whining about that. Oh, yeah, and I have to go to the allergist after that.

So maybe I'm a bit sensitive in Mexico. There is no touchstone, no standard for how I sound, or what impression I'm making. We were visiting his cousin in Chiapas, about ten years ago. His cousin teaches sociology and economics at the university there. He had an adorable eight-year-old daughter who kept smiling at me with her big black eyes and dimples in her cheeks. I asked why she kept grinning at me and Alberto, Amado's cousin, said, "She's never heard bad Spanish before." So much with my "A Level Fluency" with Los Angeles Schools.

I struggled for thirteen years, just knowing whether to use "usted" for my mother-in-law when everyone else in the family used "tu." She would always tell me (in Spanish) to use whatever I wanted, but in Mexico people have to be polite, even though, according to Amado, they don't really mean it. People say "Esta es su casa," meaning, "This is your house." I always took them at their word, and felt I could visit them and stay as long as I wanted. Amado told me that this wasn't the case. In Mexico people ask for "un poquito de agua" (a little bit of water) instead of a glass of water. If you don't ask for just a little bit of something, even in a restaurant where you're paying for it, it's rude. I can't ask for a cup of coffee in Mexico when I want one. It has to be "a little bit of coffee," "a little bit of bread," "a little bit of your attention for just a little minute." This feels hugely dishonest to me, so I'm rude. Period. They think we're rude.

I once got in a fight with Amado in Baja, because he called an officer on the toll road "joven" (young man). I thought it was condescending, but he said that it would have been rude to call him "señor." Go figure.

When I met Amado he was living with an elderly couple from Mexico, and the woman's name was Elisa. I had heard about Elisa before I met her. Months after we met she told me she really liked her son-in-law because he always called her "Sra. Sanchez." That had never occurred to me. There I go again. Rude.

Amado supposedly speaks very good Spanish. I didn't know that until many people told me. I was always suspicious because of his superiority to the conventions of English, which he thought were inconsistent and stupid. He also never knows the word I'm looking for in Spanish. His degree in physics didn't require a lot of outside vocabulary.

What drives me craziest in Spanish is the "unreal conditional" or the "subjunctive mode;" I don't remember the difference. They have to do with sentences like, 'If only I had gotten here sooner I would have gotten a seat." I need to use this mode a lot when speaking about my feelings regarding foreign policy and religion. I failed the conversational component of the state bilingual certification test with that one. I went right there. The question was something about what I would do if I were teaching in such and such a situation. I became instantly stupid and dug myself into a grammatical hole from which I couldn't extricate myself.

They say "Love knows no language;" well, I say that's hogwash. When you're calling someone by the wrong name, making him "less than" or making an insulting faux pas with the best of intentions, love knows language and waits skittishly in the doorway, holding your hat and coat, waiting for you to call it "tu" instead of "usted" or to violate a custom held sacred by your hosts. Love can be very touchy. I know how I feel when Amado says after wine and dessert, "Come lay down next to me." I'm an English teacher for Chrissake. "It's LIE down, Amado!"

Mexico is not the land of magic and romance, like they say in the travel posters. It's the land of reflexive verbs, gender and *por* versus *para.* Two different words for *for,* for God's sake, and after fifty years I still don't know which one to choose. I fell in love with the romance, the kick-back lifestyle, the piña coladas; but I married reality, which has verbs, relationships, and family, and the debilitating struggle of trying to pronounce my "r"s with my mouth full.

29 HAPPY

My cholesterol is way up and I have a slight irregularity with my EKG. I am an adult now, someone to be listened to, and someone to be reckoned with. I twist off the tops of the carrots, slice off the ends and put them in a green vase. If I tilt my head to the left I can see them in the kitchen, past Amado's flowers from Whole Foods, splayed clumsily in a crystal ice bucket (Rosemary wanted us to have *something* pretty). I love myself for the carrot tops and Amado for his flower arrangement that looks like a fiber optic lamp. I even love the mess. Miles Davis said, "It's not that I like mess, it's just that I do it so well."

The cat's quiet for once. I kept spraying her with Bach Flower Remedies so she'd stop her ugly noise. It's not a meow. It's a dissonant creaky noise. An old iron ship's door with spoiled, unpleasant "sufrida" overtones. "Sufrida" means "one who suffers" in Spanish.

The birds are chirping and I hear wind chimes. There are no pretty bird songs here in Venice. We have seagulls, sparrows, crows, and a flock of parrots that squawk insults as they fly overhead. I don't really blame them, but here the wind chimes do what birds traditionally do. Champa, my black lab, is on the floor looking at me, waiting for directions, her eyes rolled up with white half-moons underneath, like a gorilla's. The rocker from the yellow rocking chair is poised over her toe, but she knows she's safe with me.

The sun is getting lower and the beach mist is preparing to end my afternoon. I notice the floor is losing its light patches. I was beginning to worry that my happiness might set with the sun when the doorbell rings and the UPS man is there with a belt I bought for Amado and a pair of sweatpants for me. Christmas happens randomly now that I have Amazon. The sweatpants are huge and soft and luxurious with just a little elasticity, and they are gray. It always seems like a good idea to buy gray when I'm buying something new. New things make the impending dark seem not so bad.

30 MY DAD'S HEAD

My dad's head has been sitting on a chair in the dining room. Amado, my husband broke it. Well, he knocked it off its base. Amado breaks things that are in his way. He knocks into them. All things are in his way. But this time it's my father's head.

Marcus, an old friend, called a few years ago and said that Alex Kritchef's family had my father's head in their garage, and they thought that I might want it. What could I say? I drove to their house and they handed it to me. It was life-size, and green, like old copper. It was an amazing likeness. It was my father, on a pedestal.

I carried it home and put it on a shelf in my living room. It looked at me philosophically, one eyebrow slightly raised, lips pursed, with Einstein's bushy mustache. Deep in thought, it watched me watch TV.

My daughter wants it, but won't take it when she's here. It's been five years now. I called The Southern California Library of Social Research, thinking they might want it, but they're closed on Mondays, and I didn't want to leave a message. This situation requires some explanation, and I didn't know my party or extension. I don't want to give them money at this time, just the head. I gave it to my ex-husband. He was delighted. But it came back to me several months later. He asked if I knew the ear was chipped. Yes, I did, but now the other one's chipped too.

I can't screw the pedestal back in. I just tried. He's looking obliquely at the corner of the ceiling, ghastly green, and lifeless as a fish, but patient, philosophical, and nonjudgmental. I need to go into the kitchen to check the rice in the oven. I turn it to face the wall. Am I wrong, or does he look petulant?

31 ABE'S SON'S BIRTHDAY PARTY

Abe's son was 45 years old yesterday, and had spent most of his adult life in jail for credit card fraud. He got out last June, and decided to become a paralegal. He had studied a lot and had gotten a lot of experience. His only problem was a lack of references on the outside. Abe and his wife, Brenda, were a bit skeptical, but wanted to be supportive at the same time. They thought he should be a bit more practical, and maybe a bit more humble. But much to everyone's amazement he landed a wonderful job that paid $50,000 a year. That's when Abe decided to throw him a birthday party.

The invitations went out with a photo of Abe's son at 10 wearing a party hat. Stacy, their daughter, was flying down from Portland with the baby; Brenda's sister was coming up from San Diego with her husband. Family, and those who loved the family, were invited. A week later Abe's son decided to quit the job because it didn't pay enough for all the work he put in, but the party was still on. The guests showed up at 4:00, give or take a couple of hours, with brightly colored packages.

Jerrie, a friend of the family, was there with her daughter and grandson. It was her first time out since her husband, a dentist, had killed himself. She was being wonderful and brave and dressed very chic, since she worked at a clothing store for adult women. She had dyed her hair crimson. I admired that most of all. We were all careful not to say anything that might upset her.

I'd gotten the present for Abe's son through my cousin, whose son had gotten into trouble with the law for selling medical marijuana, but was doing much better and was working at Brooks Brothers. Her son wasn't able to get a discount, but they mailed me something for Abe's son anyway. I wanted to be generous, because Abe had always been so generous with us.

Stacy's baby was adorable. Stacy was Brenda and Abe's only daughter. The two sons were from a former wife who was nuts.

The other son, not the one with the birthday, the one who didn't just get out of prison (well he had been in prison, but that was a long time ago and he's doing fine now) (well, maybe not completely fine, because he still has some issues, naturally), was there with his wife and two kids—Tony, who was doing much better, and the new baby, Madison was absolutely adorable. Anyway, Abe's older son, the one with the birthday, was there with an old friend (who fell asleep in the car) but that's neither here nor there.

Amado dropped me off at a chic card shop on Main Street in Santa Monica. I had a lot of trouble finding the right card. They all said things like, "Shoot for the Moon and you'll reach the Stars" but that's what got the son arrested in the first place. Amado was to circle the block while I got the card. He must have circled for half an hour. I finally found something benign. It was about having good fortune. I couldn't find anything about working hard and staying out of trouble. That would have been nice. At least the card wasn't ghastly with bunnies and crap.

We arrived about an hour late. Amado disappeared out the back door and Brenda asked me what I'd like to drink. I asked for my usual—Crystal Light and a shot of tequila. Brenda opened up her kitchen drawer, and there were more flavors of Crystal light to choose from (outside of Gelson's) than I had ever seen before. Brenda mixed the orange Crystal Light in water, and then started pouring the tequila. "That's an awful lot of tequila," I said. "That's not a shot, Brenda." "Maybe you'd better stop pouring, Brenda...Brenda!" I drank it anyway. I didn't want to be rude...plus it was good (and sugar-free).

Dinner was excellent. I had a very small piece of chicken and two flavors of Haagen-Dazs: Rum Raisin and

Mocha Chip. There was also vanilla, but why would anyone want vanilla? The white chocolate chip cookies and regular chocolate chip cookies could easily be confused with the oatmeal raisin, which were too sweet, but I kept eating them to resolve the dilemma.

Abe made a speech, which I missed because I was in the bathroom. Abe is a contractor, and they just spent a fortune remodeling and have a guest bathroom off the family room with a pedestal sink, fancy soap, and finger towels. The family room has a bar and a huge TV screen with TiVo.

While I was in the bathroom and Abe was making a speech, Amado, who is no stranger to wine, especially someone else's wine (and I saw him ask someone to pass the bottle again for "a little bit more"), started to cry, because he didn't have a relationship with his son. Amado had had a horrific divorce where the custody battle was waged over a five-year-old and Amado was broken by their lawyer and lost. Amado's son was brought up to believe that Amado was dangerous and should be avoided at all costs. But anyway, Amado was crying a lot, and being comforted, first by Abe, then by Brenda's sister, who hadn't seen her son in many years because he's schizophrenic and on the streets somewhere. She thought Amado could use some counseling.

I didn't know how sympathetic I should be. I had to drive home. I kind of have a rule about sympathy. It goes like this: when you stop feeling sympathetic, there's probably a reason. My reason was that Amado didn't cry like that when there was no wine involved, and I'm an equal opportunity sympathizer. He had to have cried equally under sober conditions to get my sympathy. I also prefer when people don't cry in public, then get sympathy and counsel from ladies who have problems of their own.

So Abe's son got to our gift, opened the card, and smiled warmly (I guess they don't have too many birthday parties on the inside) and then he opened the gift and said, "Oh, Brooks Brothers!" when he saw the box. That was the desired effect. He took out a shirt and tie (I had hoped $100 would have gotten more, but there was no discount). I did want to look good in front of Brenda and Abe. Then he took out another card and said, "This isn't for me." I ran around the table to see what was going on. There was a pretty flowered card that said, "He was able to get the discount" and there was a $25.00 check made out to me. I told him he could keep it, that I'd endorse it, but he gallantly shook his head.

32 MONARCH

A few weeks ago I heard a scuffling sound, like a hen off its balance. I left my computer, ran into the dining room, and saw that my cat was after a Monarch butterfly. I started yelling, "No!" at her. Champa, my black lab, came slinking into the room with her tail between her legs, assuming I was yelling at her. The cat ran out. I threw the window open to let the Monarch escape, but instead, trapped her between the panes (I assumed it was a "she." Aren't most trapped things?).

My dog is gone now. I didn't know if I could bear it, putting her to sleep. Being there. I told her we were going to make her sleep so it wouldn't hurt any more. It was May eighth. She was eleven and a half.

My husband and I came home from the vet and there was a Monarch butterfly on the patio. Amado said he had never seen one like that (even though they gather in their most spectacular displays in Morelia, Mexico, a few hours from where he grew up). I had never seen one in Venice, where we live, either. It was perched on a loquat tree that I planted last year, after having a dream about a loquat tree planted there. The butterfly fluttered closer to me, and into my face, so I backed up and ran toward the patio gate. It then fluttered off to the bougainvillea, where it perched on a high stem, bordering my house and my neighbor's. My husband asked, "Do you think it's Champa?" I didn't answer—I just left the yard and got into the Prius. I'm not quite spiritual enough to think that, and not atheistic enough to dismiss it. I left it flapping on the bougainvillea.

33 SOMEWHERE OVER GREENLAND
(4:45 AM, L.A. Time)

It's so predictable that when someone attracts my attention in an airport and I detest that person beyond all reason, I am experiencing the essence of the person who's about to be sharing my armrest for the next eleven and a half hours. This small, unpleasant looking man—who reminded me of my husband's ex-boss— came scuttling into the Frankfurt airport, about 5 AM, butting in front of me. "Engineer," I thought, "or physicist. Sees people as objects that might get in one's way."

He was wearing a dress shirt with vertical gray and blue stripes, dirty tennis shoes, and was wheeling a cheap, gray carry-on. He had on large aviator glasses and his black hair was neatly parted on the side.

(If the flight attendant says, "duty-free shopping" again I might do something anti-social, something violent maybe, but I'm not awake enough to think of anything.)

Sure enough, when I am trying to make the connection at Heathrow, and my plane is supposed to be leaving in five minutes, who should whiz by me, his carry-on rattling, bumping my shoulder bag as he goes?

My new bedfellow waited until I was comfortable, and then he appeared. 35D. I got up for him to take his space in the middle seat next to me. I was on the aisle. When he hoisted his carry-on into the bin he nicked my elbow with it and stepped on my toe. I said, "Ow!" but he didn't seem to notice. I felt like smacking him already, but I didn't do anything. We had a whole ocean to cross, smashed together, and I didn't want to start off on the wrong foot, so to speak. When he finally took his seat he fidgeted a lot, nervously, almost arrogantly arranging his things.

When I was fifteen, I went to visit relatives in Washington, and when it was time for my summer school to start, my mother put me on a Greyhound bus, bound for Burbank, California, where my father was supposed to pick me up. I had the aisle seat. The window seat was taken by a man who said he was in a country western band. He had a haggard, cowboy look, with boots and a hat. He looked like he had done his share of smoking, drinking, and staying out late at night. We chatted some. It was a long ride, over a thousand miles. What I remember most, being unsupervised with a couple of dollars in my wallet, was the Lorna Doone cookies I bought at the bus stop, the feeling of being on the edge of a sleazy world, and the best it had to offer was Lorna Doone cookies. I never ate them again. I also remember the desperation from the boredom that seemed like it had no beginning, and would never end. I ached from boredom, fatigue, and queasiness, and the proximity of this cowboy who looked like a bit player from "Gunsmoke."

Somewhere between the Lorna Doones and Burbank he fell asleep, first with his head on the window, which was fine with me. Then we went around a bend, and he was on my shoulder like a burlap bag filled with bones and cigarette butts. I couldn't escape because all the seats were filled, and even if I could, I was afraid of the intimacy of just connecting with him enough to tell him he was on my shoulder. So I sat, paralyzed, for what seemed like hours. Maybe it was.

So here I was at fifty-something, trying very hard to stay in my twenty square inches of space. It's hard to combine boredom, fatigue and stress, but intercontinental flights create a hybrid environment, akin to hospitals, that brews that perfect cocktail. We had our seatbelts on. The PA system told us that the outside temperature was sixty-two degrees.

I ordered a vodka and orange juice with my last five Euros, and the flight attendant didn't have change. She kept my last euro. I was hoping that she would remember to give it back. It was a long flight, and I had maxed out my credit card and I wanted my euro. She gave me the little bottle of vodka and a plastic cup of orange juice, and a cup of ice, and a little bag of pretzels. I tried to reach for my hand sanitizer in my purse under the front seat, but I couldn't move very well. I tried to grip it with my toes while reaching sideways. I didn't want to risk any more germs than I had to breathing all that recycled air but if I could properly sanitize my hands, the pretzels and vodka could entertain me for at least fifteen minutes, and the flight was eleven and a half hours. I must have tried too hard because the cup of orange juice disappeared behind the tray, and when I tried to retrieve it, the ice disappeared. I was sitting on ice.

The fasten-seatbelt sign wasn't off yet and my pants were wet. I got up and found the cups on the floor, one inverted on top of the other, but most of the liquid had gone into the side pocket of my purse. I tried to clean out my purse with the blanket, which was mostly wet anyway. 35D stared straight ahead. While I was cleaning my purse I knocked my glasses into the aisle, and there wasn't enough space to bend down and get them. A handsome young German who was passing handed them to me.

I sat down, putting the wadded wet blanket under my feet. Then my "United Hemispheres" slipped to the floor. I contorted to get it between two fingers on my left hand.

The food came, and the food server picked up the magazine for me. I had my complimentary meal consisting of salad, appetizer, a choice of hot entrée and dessert, plus a magazine; something to do for fifteen more minutes, maybe half an hour. In another nine hours I would receive the pre-arrival meal.

My soft briefcase and purse weren't both fitting under the seat in front of me, so I was trying to maneuver them with my toes, inadvertently knocking my eye drops into the aisle. 35D started picking his teeth and smacking his lips. He then said he had to go to the bathroom. After all I'd been through he wanted me to move. He took my food tray and put it on top of his, and we parted—he going to the bathroom in the rear, I joining the line in the center, where there wasn't enough room to stand. So I had to crouch in front of seat number 13C.

A middle-aged Middle Eastern woman butted in front of me, but when the door finally swung open, she looked at me as if to say, "Were you next?" and I forgave her, and went in front of her, cleaning the whole bathroom before I left. This took at least five minutes, leaving me only about nine and a half hours to go.

I took the two melatonin that Amado had given me. "When in Rome" was the movie that was playing, starring Kristen Bell. The sound had a lot of static and I had to hold both sides of the earphones in to get any sound in my left ear. She picked a magic coin from a fountain in Rome, and many over-acting suitors were desperate to win her over. It was uncomfortable to watch, craning my neck up and to the right, holding in both earphones and listening to static.

I looked through "United Hemispheres." Apparently the Royal Botanic Gardens in Sydney, "lush with exotic plants like the Wollemi Pine" could help shake off jet lag.

I tried to do the crossword puzzle, then took a Benadryl. There was a ten-letter word for "museum" that started with an "R". Maybe it was an "S." My sinuses bothered me and my head felt heavy, but not heavy enough for sleep. After about an hour I took one of Amado's Ambiens. Finally I slept, wet, twisted and arthritic.

I finally woke as the plane was landing and we had to sit up and fasten our seatbelts. I had obviously missed the pre-arrival meal. This made me feel worldly because it's not easy for me to bypass free food—I'm cheap, plus a chronic member of Weight Watchers, and free food while traveling, I decided long ago, doesn't count. I must have looked like one of the zombies from "Night of the Living Dead," an ashen and dry-mouthed hag. We landed with a few bounces and screeched to a halt.

They turned off the air conditioner and the passengers started filing into the aisles, staring at the back of the plane. I ignored the engineer. I had spent the night next to him and didn't want to make eye contact with him. I was repelled by the intimacy we shared, even if it was just an armrest. In single file they came, ghastly and empty-eyed. It was then that I did something that I had only dreamt about. I took out the vomit bag from the little pouch and I threw up my dinner, with everybody watching, then rolled up the end, made a nice seal and staggered to the exit, crimped and dazed, dragging my damp belongings in my left hand, and the little bag in my right, as if it were a designer clutch from Bloomingdales.

34 FAME

"I support the striking coal miners, but will the striking coal miners support me?"
-Rene Richard

Many people in my family are famous, and those who aren't are annoyingly accomplished, but fame for me has always been secondhand, and like secondhand smoke it has filled my lungs without my ever having the sophistication to light up.

I haven't been very involved in my family's accomplishments. I sang once at one of my uncle's concerts at the Unitarian Church in Santa Monica. He had written a song with my dad that became pretty popular, so my friend, Mirra thought it might be nice if I sang it at one of my uncle's tributes. It was a glorious moment for me. I had been included.

I performed a few times as a kid, in events my dad put together. Everyone in the family participated, except for my mother who didn't seem to feel the need. Most of the family parties turned into hootenannies, with everyone fighting for center stage, and I waited to be asked. Actually, I'm still waiting. I always felt it was impolite to fight to be heard, that if people really wanted to hear me, I'd know about it.

My cousin Perry, who's actually a famous jazz clarinetist, mentioned me in his autobiography. I was so pleased to appear in print. I actually wrote a page of memories, and my perspective on Perry's greatness.

I took two of my brother Alan's improvisational acting workshops. When he told me I did well, or laughed when I was performing, I wagged like a cocker spaniel, feeling manipulative, like I somehow coerced him into acknowledging me.

I sang on one of my brother Bob's records. He was putting together a demo album, and used a lot of the free talent that circulated in and around our parents' house. There was my roommate, Vlatka, in a classically trained contralto on the song "Moon Shadows"; Bonnie White, a marvelous jazz singer on "I Been Around"; and me, singing soprano on "Slippin' On Down" and "Melancholy Alley". Bob actually goosed me when I was supposed to hit high A in "Slippin' On Down," and then kept the resulting "note" on the record. When I heard myself on "Melancholy Alley" in the studio I knew I was going to finally become famous. My pitch, timing—everything— was spot on. My voice sounded rich and resonant. I was the bomb. Then we got it home and played it on my parents' stereo and I sounded like Minnie Mouse, but not in a good way. Back to square one.

When my father was dying of cancer I went to visit him, bringing a new friend along. When he found out my friend's brother was a DJ, Dad asked me to play a demo tape that I had made of some songs he had written with a friend of mine, a fabulous guitarist that I had introduced him to. When I put the tape on, my voice had been erased and Bonnie White's had been dubbed in. I yelled at this twig-thin dying man. He was baffled. This is the sum total of me tapping into my family's fame.

For me to talk a lot about my family feels like name dropping, so to write about my life (the only subject of which I have any expertise) feels cheap. The most famous person in my family has got to be my brother, Alan. Alan was born a superstar. He had a machine that made phonograph records when I was very small (he left home when I was five). I don't know what machine Alan used, but he recorded an album at 18, and this album was part of my childhood mythology. I listened to music a lot. We didn't have a TV. My grandparents had one next door, and I remember going there to watch the Ed Sullivan Show or Sid Caesar, but at home I listened to music: 78s. There was Stravinsky's Firebird (Alan narrated the story for me as the music played). We had Danny Kaye, Marais and Miranda, Slim Gaillard, Pete Seeger, my uncle Earl, and my brother.

Because I saw my brother as my own personal celebrity I'd ask him from time to time to perform for my classmates. No one else ever brought in a family member for Show and Tell. He was always gracious about it, too. He never once told me to leave him the hell alone.

When Alan wasn't being a famous musician he was winning first place in ceramics competitions, photography expositions, and appearing on TV as a teenager when he won the Spade Cooley talent contest, so when he started being played on the radio it only seemed natural.

When I was about nine years old, my father and I were listening to the Hit Parade. They were doing the top ten countdown. We hadn't heard my brother's "The Banana Boat Song" yet, and we felt sad that it was history already. It wasn't number 10, 9, 8 or 7, but we still listened, getting gloomier by the minute (feeling something like I do today when losing at Words with Friends for the fiftieth time, only worse). I was sitting on the Formica kitchen counter, and my dad was at the yellow Formica table, *at* the head, where the wall-mounted ironing board, on other days, would, from time-to-time, open up and slam him *on* the head.

We listened to the entire countdown, not talking much. We couldn't believe that Elvis made the top ten, but not my big brother. They started building the drama for number one. I gripped the countertop hard and stared at the refrigerator. I heard "Hill and gully rider, hill and gully" and when I landed, my dad and I grabbed each other and started jumping around, screaming.

After that, Alan's success and fame seemed to escalate. I stopped rejoicing in his fame, and started seeing it as an affront to my lack of fame. I started feeling that way around my Uncle Earl who had won an academy award for the song "The House I Live in" that Frank Sinatra sang in a movie short, and all the published people in the family, extending my hurt to most of Hollywood, who obviously pushed their fame in my face.

To this day I prefer foreign films, preferably with actors I don't know, who have faces I've never seen before. (People also don't seem so phony when I don't understand what they're saying.)

I started giving away books that were autographed with loving notes to me. My cousin Emily wrote a book about Mae West. That went to a friend who was working on her sexuality. My sister-in-law's books went to the middle school where I was teaching. My Uncle Joe's books went to a leftist friend who was studying psychiatry. My Uncle Carl's book went to a friend who was studying interior design.

Then my dad, who had seemed to fail at his dreams (this was some comfort for me) published not two, but three books, and had one of his songs (he had always written) hit number one on the charts.

I have always identified with the underdog. I was the one who took in stray cats, frogs, students, boyfriends. I was the one who taught at-risk youth my entire life, seeing their greatness and helping them see it. I also helped them win trophies for acting and ribbons for art. I would have championed my brother Bob, who was a classic underdog playing jazz bass—an occupation that gives him almost no money and no fame, just arthritis from walking the streets of New York for thirty-five years, carrying an instrument that's got to weigh more than he does. But Bob's not the kind of guy who would let you be on his side. If he catches you on his side he changes sides.

There was a joke circulating a few years ago about the dyslexic agnostic insomniac who used to stay up nights wondering if there was a dog. Amado upgraded it as the dyslexic altruistic insomniac who stayed up nights worrying about the under-god. Well, that was me.

Eventually I had to become my own under-god, my own underdog, so I could root for myself. I needed to keep the victories coming, but keep them coming slow, so as not to lose the identity of underdog; not sell out, otherwise I'd have to find someone else to root for.

I'm comfortable championing others. Right now it's my cat. She's pretty fat, but I know she can make it onto this chair if she really applies herself. She just looked up at me, then closed her eyes slowly, obviously fatigued. She looks irritated with me. She left for under the desk. Was she rolling her eyes at me? I know she expects more from me. Our relationship's been a disappointment to her. I put her on a diet, won't let her go out at night, or sleep with me anymore. I explained about the asthma, but she's not buying it. She thinks it's a copout. She thought I had so much promise, but I'm just like all the others.

35 ENLIGHTENMENT

I've been very annoyed about enlightenment. I didn't realize how over it I was until I started reading some enlightened magazine in the doctor's office. I used to search the pages of magazines like that, looking for the answer, just like I sometimes do on Amazon. Same principle. If I buy the product I'll look slim, serene and radiant like the people in the pictures. The only difference is that one has photographs of models, the other of practitioners. I do want to be thoughtfully blissful with good hair and blue shimmering eyes looking straight at you, and yet not. "I see that you look cranky, but, hey. Namaste."

I've been there. I've looked for God in all people. But why is someone who's a cranky pain in the ass less of a teacher than the misty-eyed professional guru?

I saw my yoga teacher yelling at her kids in the parking lot on Ventura Boulevard, just behind the yogurt place. She was dragging the little boy by one arm. She had been a goddess the evening before, flexible with a voice like an angel and infinite patience.

It is overwhelming and appalling to hear about politics or the environment as well. I soon feel like the world is going to hell fast, and it's essentially my fault. I didn't grow up seeing starving polar bears, Civil War in Uganda, or knowing about 500,000 animals killed annually in California shelters.

I'm walking a tightrope between "God is all there is" and "It's all going to hell in a hand basket." The two ideas are contradictory and seem only to be resolved with compassionate detachment, or maybe drugs.

It's not productive to say, "You're shitting on this magnificent planet, you asshole," and then call yourself spiritual. Maybe you can say, "You're shitting on this beautiful planet, my brother."

When I filled up my car at Chevron on Lincoln and Venice there was a woman behind me with a black SUV. She smiled at me and said, "Seventy-one dollars and I still didn't fill it!" I smiled back. I wanted to say, "Fuck you. Serves you right." Maybe next time you'll buy a Prius.

Change is inevitable. The planet as we know it is coming to an end. Global warming is a fact. Bengal tigers are becoming extinct. Big Bear is losing its trees. Trump is in the White House but all's well with the world.

36 HONORABLE DISCHARGE

I'm at the Tamaya Resort and Spa in Bernalillo, New Mexico. I've just finished my breakfast. It was perfect. There's a spectacular view out the window, a perfect desertscape with cobalt sky, sand and cumulous clouds. I'm in a corner booth. The Navajo theme is fairly consistent, but right now something that sounds like the Gypsy Kings is playing on the PA system. That doesn't really bother me. The thing that keeps bothering me is the amount of phlegm coming out of so few people here. Only four tables are occupied and there is phlegm coming from three of them.

The man sitting in the booth in front of mine keeps blowing his nose—even worse, sucking it in, and coughing. He's wearing a plaid, button-down collared engineer shirt. His gray hair curves moistly in several directions on the back of his neck. Across the room, silhouetted against the craggy bluffs, are three dark women, one with short gray hair. I think she's the one with all the phlegm, but I can't be sure. I keep hearing throat clearing, snorting in, and loose coughing.

I'm using the leftover Kleenex from the airplane. I'm much more discreet. I would never snort it in at the table (or anywhere, really). I blow my nose gently. It doesn't interfere with my appetite at all, but I have to really focus here to finish my poached eggs, little fruit cup instead of potatoes, coffee with Splenda, soy milk, and hot wheat toast in a basket with a burgundy cloth napkin covering it to keep in the heat. You can really hear the Moorish influence in that piece that's probably the Gypsy Kings.

Why am I at Tamaya Resort and Spa in Bernalillo, New Mexico? My husband, Amado is here for a classified conference about unmanned aircraft. Even he doesn't know where they're going to take him. Last night I ate and drank at the reception. The drinks were free, and Amado and I each had a few. Amado started leaning towards his colleague who was sitting on his right at our round table. She was pretty, Asian, and in her thirties. She also had a PhD. I was being ignored. This was not so good for me that evening. After the reception Amado and I went to the parking lot to get our luggage to bring up to our rooms. He opened his mouth to say something to me and my fist went out and I slugged him in the solar plexus. I didn't do a lot of damage, but he was surprised, and so was I.

There were a lot of military people at the hotel, but I don't believe in war. I don't think unmanned aircraft can protect us from the takeover of this, the Bush administration for instance, who seem to be as big a threat to our country as any I could think of. I love my husband. I love his warm body at night, his hairy chest, his devotion to me. I worry about abandoning my principles, loving a man who does work for the military. No, I am abandoning my principles. I wonder about other women who sleep with the enemy, Pan's Labyrinth, Spain, Germany, Italy, Vietnam. There we have always been, the women who love the men who buy us nice things with money from unmanned aircraft, listening to what might be the Gypsy Kings, wondering about the yoga class, learning to meditate, to go within, to not judge, to love ourselves unconditionally, and everyone else, unconditionally, trying to get out of our heads in New Mexico, and around the world. We hold hands, and dance, my spirit sisters, in spas, everywhere.

37 MEXICO

I've had a head cold for over a week now. When I bend over I hear my heart beating (next to mine). Breathing has become fully absorbing. I feel like a stranger here. People seem distant, and relating to them is too much effort. I know the precise moment I got this cold, and I made the conscious decision to act on what should be instead of what was.

My husband and I were visiting his family in Mexico City for New Years. I am the only Gringa, and it is very important to me that they think of me as one of them—a real Mexican. I stop only at eating red meat. Other than that, I'm their girl. I'm ten years older than my husband, I'm divorced (twice) and I'm the daughter of Jewish Communist Atheists, so I don't have a lot of room to play here. My Spanish is excellent for the classroom, Mexican restaurants or seaside resorts, but at a family gathering I usually just concentrate on the potato chips.

I had been told that Aunt Carmina made the traditional pork dish out of chicken, to honor me. Right after midnight, Lalo, my husband's ex-brother-in-law offered me a taco made from this very chicken. Now, several years ago Amado invited this ex-brother-in-law to come to the U.S. with Amado's sister to take a personal growth course that we had taken, because their marriage was in trouble, and it had done wonders with ours. She came alone, took the course, then booted poor Lalo out of the house. A few years later we took their daughter, Samantha, in for a year; now here he was, telling me, with tears in his eyes, how grateful he was.

Just after midnight Lalo looked at me with pale, dejected eyes, asking me if I would like him to get me that taco. If I had said no, I would not have been rejecting just Lalo, nor merely Amado's entire family, but Mexico itself. I would have been a Gringa: superior, spoiled, closed, and antiseptic. It was at this point that I noticed there was a pool of moisture barely discernible just under Lalo's left nostril.

I froze for a moment. There was so much at stake, but then I decided, "Oh, what the hell! It's New Years and I'm in Mexico with my Mexican family who have learned to love and accept me in spite of the fact that Polk invaded and innumerable historical miserable acts that should have made them spit at me and my *pinche* Gringo roots.

When I was about 14 years old I went to Ensenada with my parents. We were walking down the street when some young Mexican guy yelled, "Yanqui go home!" My father said, "Yes! You're right!" and nodded with approval. I tried to drag him away saying, "They're talking about us, Dad!" "I know," he replied. "They're right!"

So I ate the taco and the twelve grapes at midnight, and tried to sing the old songs from Mexico and Spain that I didn't know, and we danced until six or seven, and everyone slept in but me.

And now I drink Gripte, my favorite Mexican cold remedy, and take decongestants in two languages, whine, and refuse to go out or do any work. But I'm back in

California. My reputation seems to be intact, and laying aside all the awful things our country has done, I'm so lucky to be home.

38 SIXTY

When I was young life was simple. There were certain truths about the world, and we conformed to these truths: we were Jews. There was no God. Communism was good. My teachers and friends weren't bad, just not well informed, and if I were smart enough or knowledgeable enough I could explain what was right to them, they would change their minds, and all would be well. They'd be on the right side. The government was bad. The Soviet Union was good, and so was Cuba. But China wasn't so good.

This was the world. Now about me: I could do many things, but I was lazy, disorganized, an operator, a whiner (all this according to my mother), had hairy legs and bad hair, my feet and neck were dirty, and I was black. I wasn't actually black, but I had been told I was by a neighborhood child who used the "N" word. I believed I was perceived as black. My mother had told me I was Caucasian for the purpose of applications, but it seemed dishonest. If Ozzie and Harriet were Caucasians, if the Mouseketeers were Caucasian, then I wasn't. This is how it was. My grandparents thought I was wonderful, and my grandfather worried about me. They lived next door. Some of my relatives seemed annoyed by me, and others seemed to like me okay. I wanted everyone to like me, but never figured out the trick.

Nowadays life is still simple: I try to stay in the present moment; if I don't I get hysterical. My form of hysteria is internal and appears to the outside world as if I were calm and perhaps indifferent. The present moment looks like this:

I may have to go to the bathroom my desk is a mess that's okay oh, there's my book maybe I should read it Amado thinks I should read it in Spanish the hell with that just type I need to fix the curtain the dog needs her flea meds she needs to be washed first.

I realize now that if everyone liked me, my life could get very crowded, and I'd have more time-management problems than I already do.

The temperature is now 62.4 degrees. It was 61-point-something when I lit the fireplace. I know L.A.'s supposed to be warm, but here by the beach it's damp, and the house is drafty. Maybe I will go to the bathroom. I'll escape any way I can. Nope. I won't. I'll confront my life.

I'm sixty. No one can believe it. They say I look much younger, and apparently I act immature, which used to be an insult, but now seems to be a good thing. I may appear younger, but I feel solidly Boomer.

I lived through drop drills. I was going to be blasted to smithereens by the Soviet Union who couldn't see that, on the first floor of Buchanan Street School, I, too, was a Communist. I was their comrade. What my government did wasn't my fault. Nothing much in that sense has changed.

I also lived through sit-in demonstrations at the Board of Ed to integrate schools in Los Angeles. I lived through peace marches too, and love-ins. My mother called me a Hippie, but I always worked and/or went to school, set my hair, and wore makeup. I did write poetry and smoke pot, however.

My first husband was in a blues band. He married me because I walked out on him, because he didn't know if he'd want to marry me when he became a famous rock and roll star. He bought me a huge bouquet of flowers and said he would have gotten me a puppy, but he didn't have enough time. I had to marry him. I was 21, and sex was great. I realized there were orgasms coming from him, and I wanted to keep them permanently. Besides, the word "puppy" disarmed me.

He was in a great blues band that disbanded because the harp player from Muddy Waters' band told them they sounded white. The lead singer quit and moved to Oregon. That was that. Annette, my best friend, fell in love with the lead guitarist and her face matched whatever the guitar was doing. If he'd play a solo and there were high notes, her eyebrows would follow the riffs. We used to sit there while they practiced.

I heard Kennedy speak at an NAACP rally before he was president. He was booed and I felt bad for him. I always felt stupid being part of a group, chanting too. "Hell, no, we won't go." Or singing, "We Shall Overcome." Much of what embarrassed me then makes me cry now, for the same reasons it embarrassed me then. We were so full of hope and idealism. Could I have been a cynic already, back then, even though I tried so hard not to be?

What have I learned, really, that I can contribute to the world, now that I get a senior citizen's discount at Ross on Tuesdays?

What I've learned is this: a messy desk is it. It's the promise, the glory, the passion, the love and the beauty. It's all that life has to offer. It's my desk. I won't always have it. I won't always have these hands to type on my new Apple keyboard cover that keeps food out of the keyboard. I also won't always have these same wrinkled hands that used to fill me with sadness, because, even when I was ten years old they looked wrinkled. I'm so grateful to have these little, wrinkled, olive-green hands on this keyboard cover, with a manicure that Cute Nails does perfectly now.

I'm grateful for the body that I would have been jealous of back then. I'm now jealous of many things I had back then. But that part of me might be envious of me now. I am thankful to have a life that can be envied, even if just by my former self, for my messy desk, in my imperfect house in Venice, with its problems, and my splintery wood floor, and the 64.0 degrees (it's getting warmer) and my Weight Watchers book, and Gal Costa CD and Marquez, with an accent over the "A" and Mexican coasters, and the sun shining on Francene's peeling house next door, and the banana tree, and Marcus's ceramic pot and the coupons, and Amado, my husband, my dog, my cat, my kids, my agent, my producers, and the whole academy.

39 BRENDA

When Brenda asked me to do something for her retirement/going away party I was flattered. Brenda knows me well enough to know that I'd do just about anything for attention. And she was giving me a chance, winding me up and pointing me in her direction. We met at a *California Consortium for Independent Studies* in Palm Springs where we skipped workshops, such as *A Hands-on Approach to Addressing the Needs of the Whole Child,* to go up in a hot air balloon (the speakers were full of hot air anyway), went to a karaoke bar, and fought off Bernard, who after having a few was feeling amorous towards either one of us, or anyone else, it seemed.

We drove home together and Brenda talked about her husband Abe's grizzly beginnings. He was born in Auschwitz, it seemed, but had no records or memories to prove it. She spoke of her tennis elbow, her four hours a day of competitive playing, her two surgeries, and missing Stacy, her daughter, who was in Australia, doing her senior year kayaking and bungee jumping. If you told me then we were going to become best friends I would have told you that you were crazy.

Brenda and I lived close enough together to start carpooling, and it was then we discovered that we both wanted to learn tap dancing. Pretty soon we were studying with Jon Zerby at Everywoman's Village. John was once a Broadway dancer who was now in his 80s. He claimed to have taught Michael Flatley. He had a penchant for yelling at Brenda while we did stupid Shirley Temple routines. I never got yelled at, however. I was in my glory.

We started going to yoga together, too, then to Weight Watchers. Hermein Lee, the diet Nazi, who was also in her 80s, yelled at Brenda. I, however got down to 110 pounds (temporarily). I got mine later when I confessed that I had had some frozen yogurt, but it was sugar free. She asked me what it had in it and I replied *malt o-dextrin*, and she yelled, *What the hell do you think that is?* I miss Hermein.

Then Brenda and I started going to conferences together. It worked out well because I would go anywhere, and Brenda would do all the work. She would find the conferences, fill out the forms, send me the copies to sign (all stapled), call the conference, call the office for approval, remind me to sign and mail things. She didn't, however, send in the paperwork for me to get reimbursed, so I often got snagged up there, and sometimes would forget altogether.

After Palm Springs there was New Orleans, New York, and Nashville. We were roommates at the weekend in Oxnard too, and again in Buena Park. We drank cheap wine, called it mead, then cheered for the yellow knight at *Medieval Times*. Soon we got our husbands in on the act and we started taking longer trips...three weeks in Peru and

Bolivia, ten days in Costa Rica, San Miguel de Allende twice, and of course, Tijuana. Brenda and Abe were ready to go. They did the research, then talked us into going, because we always had intended to go somewhere else, but hadn't organized it. So Brenda and Abe would organize everything and we'd just slide into the slots they left for us.

Brenda was with me when I met Amado. I had been following Brenda to Borderline in Moorpark where she met a group of friends for line dancing. It was very hokey and contrived. I loved it. Amado selected me through a dating service and didn't want the torture of a blind date, so I asked him to meet me with Brenda and her friends, because he had said he liked line dancing. Brenda told me that she thought he was cute. I couldn't get past the cowboy hat and boots, and a face that didn't look harmonious.

When I started dating Amado, each time I felt like running for the horizon she would tell me something totally sensible and unromantic, the kinds of thoughts that had never before entered my consciousness. Being sensible was exotic to me. Brenda became my relationship guru.

Brenda is a very good friend. She never forgets anything, whether you're going to meet her for lunch or not, if it's your birthday, or if she has to pay you for tickets. She even used to bring extra cheese to faculty meetings, because she knew I sure as hell wouldn't have any with me, and one mustn't run out of cheese. When I retired, and City of Angels forgot to acknowledge me, Brenda ran to the podium, even though it terrified her, and made a speech about me. It was too short, but, hey.

I feel very bad that Brenda is choosing her grandchildren over me. Even though she promised that she has an excellent guest room, and I can take my dog when I visit, it just isn't the same. I'm starting to feel all weepy, but I don't want to cry. I'm tired of hearing how great Portland is, because it's annoying. And besides, if I'm to follow my grandchildren I'll be wearing cowboy boots in Austin before too long and calling people Ma'am. Or moving to Brooklyn if a Chihuahua counts as a grandchild.

I know Brenda's philosophy of religion is *'I don't know.'* Well, go with *"I Don't Know,"* Brenda, and may "*I Don't Know*" keep you safe. Brenda's courageous to start a new life in a new city at sixty-five. It's inspiring and life affirming. My sense of adventure these days seems limited to going to Whole Foods on a weekday, or maybe mailing a letter on Windward Circle. The man in front of the post office wants my money and I don't want to give it to him. I want him to go away. I wonder what the post office is like where they live in Portland.

40 ROAD TRIP

A few years ago I got a call from my cousin Perry.

Bonnie! Perry here. Listen! I think I have a sister. She lives in California, not too far from you, and she's a minister! I think it sounds like that same religion that you were into.

This is how I came to know Pam. She never actually had a blood test, and I don't know if she's legitimately a cousin, but she's been my cousin since that phone call. My mother's sister was married to a man who slept around a lot, so it seemed plausible. We had studied the same religion, Religious Science, and she had gone on to become a minister.

So Pam, several years later, was flying to Austin, Texas, to drive back to California with me. We decided to leave late, because it was 103 degrees out and the evening seemed best for travel, but after we dawdled and went out for coffee, I got antsy and wanted to hit the road.

We put the dog in the car with all the clothes and toiletries that I figured I'd need for the next few months.

It's twenty-two hours and five minutes from my home in Austin to Venice, California, where Amado still lives, and where I used to live full-time. When I moved to Austin I said I'd spend the summers in California. I hadn't figured out the logistics, but I made the commitment anyway.

I figured out the logistics for this trip though. We'd spend the first night in Balmorhea, Texas. Yelp had some good reviews of it. It had a spring-fed pool, the largest in the country, with fish and snakes. I didn't want to stay in Ft. Stockton, because of the bedbug bites I got the last time I stayed there, and the best place to eat in town, according to the lady behind the desk at Motel 6, was Sonic. Other than that, she said, it was all fast food.

Pam was trying to manage her church from the road. What I hadn't counted on was that the sound of her texting, and the upbeat, supportive sound of her voice would just about drive me insane. She was having cheery, loving conversations while we were passing back-breaking heat and road kill. Not just smashed, furry things, but whole deer, being eaten by vultures. That kind of road kill.

Let us now know that all will be well and so it is!

I was thinking of creating a road trip game called "Name that Animal." The gray fuzzy thing with what looked like legs in the air might be say a…coyote! Were those things legs? There were only three of them. Oh, that one was totally mashed. That fur was sort of orange. What was it? A fox? They do have foxes in Texas. Did it suffer when it was hit? If everything dies anyway does it matter whether it's smashed by a truck or starved to death?

What would be a kind death for a deer? Is it kinder for it to be killed by a predator or a hunter? Is it crueler than the death of, say, the cow, who's just raised to be slaughtered? Should I be as forgiving of hunters as I am of four-legged predators? Why do some people condemn hunting, and not feed lots, or slaughterhouses?

There is too much time for thinking on the road, and I can't stand any more of my music. I could enjoy it a bit more if Pam would listen to it, rather than heal everyone. Why can't I appreciate my own music while she's texting? I handpicked it on iTunes. Why do I need an audience?

I am an animal lover, mostly because I am an animal. Our vision of separateness from animals is vanity. It's the same separateness that we use when we want to dominate, say, a person, and take what he has. He's got different skin; I can't understand him so he's obviously not as intelligent as me. I think I'll take his land!

My religion is the only true religion, my country's the best, and so is my species, and I can prove all this by tests I've created.

When a dog creates a test, say, by challenging you to pull a rag out of his mouth, at least he gives you a chance; otherwise he seems to get bored. He likes a game with higher stakes when he makes up the rules.

We seem to think an animal is brilliant if he can compete in our world, speak our language, make us understand what he is trying to say.

I think road kill is okay, but for the sake of fairness they should leave human cadavers on the highway as well.

I was driving the Prius, praying that it held out, surrounded by blood and death, and accompanied by a very cheery church-voice. In Balmorhea, where Pam slept on top of the covers because of the bugs, she revealed to me that she didn't notice the dead deer. Maybe just one. She was too busy with the church calls, but it sure didn't stop me from seeing every last body. Pam didn't get into the bed, and I wouldn't dive into the pool with all the little fish, and the possible snakes lurking somewhere, unseen. I put my feet into the cold water and waited until the park ranger chased us out. It was dusk.

We ate at Yolanda's, who cooked for the schools. In the evening she served the townspeople out of an old trailer and closed whenever she felt like it. She made me a cheese sandwich, and Pam a hamburger. We had nowhere to sit. I found a pipe and Pam sat on the trailer hitch. The cheese sandwich was wonderful with avocado and tomatoes. She toasted the bread, torta style, and I had the fresh-squeezed lemonade that she recommended.

We spent the next two nights in Silver City, New Mexico, at an old friend's house, then set off for Phoenix, where it was supposed to be 113 degrees. We ate lunch in Tucson in the patio of a coffee shop, because we couldn't leave the dog in the car.

The thermometer kept rising as we left Phoenix, until it reached 120. Cars were stopped by the side of the highway, families bent forward, heads bowed in the scorching heat. We continued in our little air-conditioned bubble, eating almonds, while Pam talked to her congregation.

I was never so aware of what a fragile thread it is that keeps us alive: those four tires, some fiberglass, an air-conditioning vent. Pam was affirming God. I was banking on Toyota.

I Rescue Spiders

I rescue spiders.
Ignorance makes them cross over.
If I were to cross over I'd want forgiveness.

I got bit twice this summer.
I don't believe in the death penalty but
The last small bug went down the drain.

I have the right to my space.

We have entered the valley of the dragons.
Hold my hand.
Don't leave the path
Or if you do, sing
And maybe hop.

Tap Dance

I am 60
My hair curls past my shoulders.
Rivulets.
Dark curls; borrowed color.
Saucy. Not right for 60.

I'm 60
Camping hurts my back.
It always hurt my back,
But now when it does I worry
That it's going to stay that way.

Waterskiing in Tahiti.
Skimming over the lagoon on my first try.
Bikini in the tropical sun, my own tan; 116 pounds,
worrying
About the extra one
I mused that the water was ferocious
Afraid to fall and break something that won't have the
Wherewithal to mend.
Marriage was a week old and bliss was work.

I'm 60
124.5 lbs.
worrying about the extra six.
I heard gravity was the enemy of age.
The floor is my enemy.

I fell down in Texas in my skirt.
I was walking.
People came from all around.
"Are you okay?"
A young guy on a bicycle asks. Kind of cute.
"I'm humiliated," I told him.
Let me get up and walk.
Shit, don't bleed.

I am 60

Only three in the tap dance class.
Brenda's back's out.
Zelda broke her arm roller-skating.
The other Zelda's playing the saxophone in a jazz band
I can't keep up with Adonis and Carol.
"Yeah, I get it," I said, "my feet won't do it."

I'm 60
I may not be a dancer one day if I practice real hard.
I'll try singing.
Damn Adonis.

I'm 60
Bought a red dress at Loehmann's for 20 bucks.
I look hot.
Just don't lift my arms,
Because the motherfucking batwings have gotten out of
control,
And don't tell me about any triceps exercises.
I have done them all.

I am 60
I was talking to my husband while I was washing
My sinus rinse bottle.
I sprayed soapy water up into my brain.
Forgot to rinse.
I was up till 2 a.m. blowing fucking bubbles out of my
nose.
Brainwashed.
I still can't smell anything.

I'm 60
I got a magazine for people over 50 at Wild Oats.
They talked about Living Trusts and reverse mortgages.
Retiring to Mexico.
Screw that magazine.

I'm 60
Sex is getting better.
Married someone ten years younger.

Sometimes he seems so old.

I'm 60
Death is closer than it ever was; but it always is,
Isn't it?
They say stay in the present moment.
I usually do.
Don't have a choice. I forget everything anyway.

I'm 60
I love myself so tenderly; even though
I know myself all these years, I still delight in my company.
I'm happy when I see myself in mirrors, unless I look too
Close, but, hey.

I'm 60
I have a house at the beach.
I don't work. I'm besotted with my kids,
Granddaughter named Emalina Moon.
My big black dog and tortie fat cat
And I'm in love

Advice

If you're not enjoying the past or future, stay in the present.
It's all good, even bad things (Don't tell that to someone who's suffering).
Be tender to your body and your mind.
When you're feeling negative, indulge yourself.
Do everything slowly and love it.
Really look and listen.
Some of my best writing came from the DMV or faculty meetings.
Taste your food.
Experience new, even if it's the same thing.
You don't have to if you don't want to.
It's okay to want it all.
It's okay not to have it all.
Love for nothing.
The right people are in your life.
There's always enough.
It's so good to love yourself.

Made in the USA
Columbia, SC
20 February 2022